THE PRACTITIONER
HANDBOOK
for Spiritual Mind Healing

The connection between our thoughts/beliefs with our health/
life experiences has been recently heralded as an important
discovery by scientists. Yet in the 1920s Dr. Ernest Holmes
extensively studied what others had already written about this
and synthesized his understanding in *The Science of Mind* text.
He described it as a correlation of laws of science, opinions of
philosophy, and revelations of religion. The first sentence of the
text reads, *We all look forward to the day when science and religion
shall walk hand in hand through the visible to the invisible.* Today it
is very exciting that science more fully than ever before supports
the principles of this teaching.

    The Practitioner Handbook is a how-to book for students of
The Science of Mind who want to learn spiritual mind healing,
a highly effective technique for physical and mental healing. It is
based on the understanding that *we are surrounded by a Universal
Mind, which reacts to our thought—and always according to Law.* This
is introduced with an in-depth look at the Law of Cause and Effect
and how it works. The student learns methods of working with
a client to clarify the effect/experience they want to change; the
experience they want to have; and the cause or belief system that

is out of alignment with their goal. From that information, a spiritual mind treatment is created by the practitioner.

The Practitioner Handbook assists students in developing their skills in listening, inquiry, teaching principles, and creating spiritual mind treatments. Students who perfect the technique of spiritual mind treatment, complete classroom studies, and pass written and oral exams can be licensed as Practitioners at over 400 Centers for Spiritual Living, which is headquartered in Golden, Colorado. The author, Rev. Mary Mitchell, became a Licensed Practitioner in 1993, a minister in 2003, and was ordained in 2008. She is passionate about teaching *The Science of Mind* classes at the Center for Spiritual Living in Redding, California.

THE PRACTITIONER
HANDBOOK
for Spiritual Mind Healing

THE PRACTITIONER
HANDBOOK
for Spiritual Mind Healing

Rev. Mary E. Mitchell

Park Point Press
Golden, Colorado

Park Point Press
573 Park Point Drive
Golden, Colorado 80401-7402

Cover design, book layout & typesetting by
Maria Robinson, Designs On You, LLC.
Littleton, Colorado 80121
Set in 11 point Chaparral Pro

Printed in USA
Published November 2014

ISBN 978-0-917849-33-6

CONTENTS

THE PRACTITIONER'S BLESSING

The Power within me blesses all mankind, and is forever healing all with whom I come in contact. The Power within me is God and It must bless, help, and heal all who come near It.

Silently the work goes on, and silently all are being helped by this Inner Power, which is operating through me. I give thanks that this Power within is silently blessing and helping everyone to whom my thought reaches.

The Life within me blesses all mankind. And so it is.

By Rev. Mary E. Mitchell

Because the whole of Spirit is present at the point of our attention, it follows that the entire Creative Power of the universe is being individualized through that attention.

Ernest Holmes
Lessons in Spiritual Mind Healing (13)

Recently I created a class called "Science and God" to review what scientists and physicists have learned so far about how the universe works, how our body works, and, in quantum physics, how our cells work, and the power of our mind. It was fascinating, because it supports what Ernest Holmes wrote about Religious Science in *The Science of Mind* text about how the universe works and the power of our mind to impact how our cells work. As Practitioners, we know this truth makes all things possible.

Science of Mind classes help stretch our minds and increase our sense of empowerment. For instance, did you know that today most scientists believe that if life were random, it would take more time than the universe has existed just to create bacteria? Even to the most jaded scientist, the Big Bang strongly points toward a creator and some scientists say the universe looks more like a great thought than a machine. Many have concluded that wisdom is the driving force, which is why the study of how the universe operates is called metaphysical—beyond the physical. It is why the Science of Mind teaching is also called metaphysical. Ernest Holmes taught that the immanence of God is the spiritual impulse underlying all life. It is the divinity of the Universe.

In Religious Science and the Science of Mind philosophy, we talk a lot about the Law of Cause and Effect and conclude that there is a law of nature by observing the consistency between cause and effect. We derive the law of gravity by observing the motion of falling items. We observe energy transfers, such as by watching boiling water turn into steam. The cause behind the moment of creation, which is now called the Big Bang, has been debated for centuries, but we do see, feel, and experience the effect: we are living beings here on planet Earth.

What have practitioner training and effective prayer to do with how the Universe was created? Scientists currently recognize that the field of the universe is energy in motion. About fourteen billion years ago, there was a moment when an infinitely dense, dimensionless point of intense energy, electromagnetic radiation, exploded. After the Big Bang, temperatures started dropping and three of the lightest elements were formed: hydrogen, helium, and lithium. Today these elements are found throughout the universe, confirming there once was a unity of cause. Temperatures dropped further and matter began to coalesce into galaxies, but as density increased, temperatures rose until nuclear fusion created further explosions. We can see some of the super nova explosions in photos from the Hubble telescope and NASA's deep space research (www.hubblesite.org).

The combination of four hydrogen nuclei and one helium nucleus created the fuel for stars. As these elements burn, heavier elements of carbon and oxygen are generated. As stars collapse and explode, more carbon and oxygen are thrown into space. Eventually the elements clump together to form matter, and through gravitational pull, the stars and planets were formed, and through fusion, the ninety-two elements were formed.

Think about the timeline. Scientists estimate that the Big Bang occurred 14 billion years ago. Earth formed about 4 billion years ago, and eventually single-celled organisms formed. Evidence suggests that the land remained barren until about 400 million years ago when plants first appeared—370 million years ago, animals moved on to land. Just 150,000 years ago, the first Homo sapiens appeared. I remember American astronomer Carl Sagan's one year clock: if all creation occurred in one calendar year, humans would finally appear at 10:30 p.m. on December 31.

Eventually things settled down in our Milky Way galaxy, thanks to strong and weak nuclear forces, electromagnetism, and gravity. In 1929, astronomer Edwin Hubble discovered that the universe as a whole was expanding. Even distant galaxies continue to move away from each other between 5 and 10 percent every thousand million years—imagine each galaxy as a dot on a rubber balloon riding along as it expands. In a quick summary about how the universe was created, science is currently saying

» The Big Bang strongly points toward a creator;
» Wisdom is the driving force;
» The universe is stable through the constants of the speed of light, strength of nuclear forces, electromagnetism, and gravity;

» Quantum fluctuations at the subatomic level have vast repercussions in evolution; and

» The fundamental forces that brought the earth and planets together are at work in our bodies and our everyday life.

Not many years ago, we were taught that the smallest part of anything was an atom with a nucleus containing protons and neutrons, with electrons spinning around the nucleus. My favorite analogy for the size of an atom is if the nucleus of an atom was the size of an orange, the electrons would be found four miles away. Most of the atom is empty space or what looks like empty space. It is the electromagnetic forces in and between the atoms, including the recently discovered Higgs boson, that enable particles to clump together and appear as solid objects.

It wasn't until 1986 that science discovered there were particles smaller than atoms, and in 1996 physicists realized that the universe is not just made of atoms suspended in empty space. Everywhere they looked, all they found were waves of energy. All parts of an atom have an energy field with wave-like characteristics. The waves of energy keep an atom spinning, vibrating, and radiating. As scientists studied this energy, they found even smaller things they called quarks, which ended up with names like up, down, top, bottom, and charmed. Between 1985 and 1995, scientists dug deeper, and some think they may have found a unified theory for everything—string theory—vibrating strings, vibrational patterns that can loop and twist and turn. It is possible that every particle at its smallest level consists of vibrational patterns of energy. This is still a theory, but a promising one. Yet, Stephen Hawking wrote that in fifty years he believes all of this will be seen as primitive thinking.

This handbook was originally published in 2001 by myself, known then as Mary Schroeder, with Dr. James Golden, the co-pastor of the Church of Religious Science in Redding, California. I was licensed as a Practitioner in 1993. There was no printed curriculum for practitioner training at that time, so I compiled the first edition of this handbook from the copious notes I took in class, with the goal of helping other students understand how to develop an effective healing practice.

Eventually, I was licensed as a staff minister in 2002. This was followed by chaplain training and serving as a volunteer chaplain in a local hospital for several years. As time passed, Dr. James left the church to take on a new role in life. His wife, Dr. Andrea, continued as pastor of the renamed Spiritual Enrichment Center for a few years before retiring to begin a new chapter in her life. In 2006, I married my wonderful husband, Paul Mitchell, after fifteen years of being together. In 2008 I was ordained and in 2009, I accepted the role of assistant minister to our new co-pastors, Rev. Judith Churchman and Rev. Bob Luckin, at the renamed Center for Spiritual Living. When they retired in 2012, Rev. Sue MillerBorn and I accepted the roles of interim co-pastors, and we continued in that role for two years until a new senior pastor was hired.

In the past few years, the parent organizations—International Centers for Spiritual Living and the United Centers for Spiritual Living—merged and are now using a new curriculum for the Science of Mind 300 Practitioner Training Unit, developed at the Mile Hi Church in Lakewood, Colorado. After teaching this excellent class with the new curriculum and my book, I felt it was an appropriate time to update this handbook.

Practitioner training is the greatest gift we can give ourselves on the spiritual path. It is inspiring to realize that we live in a state of perpetual growth, where we learn not only about ourselves and this magnificent universe, but most importantly the role we play in the evolution of humanity and our own soul. May this handbook inspire and uplift you on this sacred journey.

Rev. Mary E. Mitchell

DECLARATION
OF PRINCIPLES OF SCIENCE
OF MIND

We believe in God, the Living Spirit Almighty; one, indestructible, absolute and self-existent Cause. This One manifests Itself in and through all creation but is not absorbed by Its creation. The manifest universe is the body of God; it is the logical and necessary outcome of the infinite self-knowingness of God.

We believe in the individualization of the Spirit in us and that all people are individualizations of the One Spirit.

We believe in the eternality, the immortality and the continuity of the individual soul, forever expanding.

We believe that heaven is within us, and that we experience it to the degree that we become conscious of it.

We believe the ultimate goal of life to be a complete emancipation from all discord of every nature, and that this goal is sure to be attained by all.

We believe in the unity of all life, and that the highest God and the innermost God is One God. We believe that God is personal to all who feel this Indwelling Presence.

We believe in the direct revelation of Truth through our intuitive and spiritual nature, and that any man may become a revealer of Truth who lives in close contact with the indwelling God.

We believe that the Universal Spirit, which is God, operates through Universal Mind, the Law of God; and that we are surrounded by this Creative Mind which receives the direct impress of our thought and acts upon it.

We believe in the healing of the sick through the Power of this Mind.

We believe in the control of conditions through the Power of this Mind.

We believe in the eternal goodness, the eternal Loving-kindness and the eternal Givingness of Life to All.

We believe in our own soul, our own spirit, and our own destiny; for we understand that the life of all is God.

Chapter 1

INTRODUCTION

Great teachers throughout the ages understood the Universe to be the result of the contemplation of Divine Mind, which created humanity out of Itself. Our individuality is a consequence of the thoughts of Divine Mind formed into images. Therefore, as God expresses through us (the result of Its consciousness), we become more conscious of our own divinity. The teachings of Jesus describe the Universe as a combination of love and law, of person and principle, of feeling and force. The Science of Mind philosophy is just as direct and clear.

> *The study of the Science of Mind is a study of First Cause, Spirit, Mind, or that invisible Essence, that ultimate Stuff and Intelligence from which everything comes, the Power back of creation—the Thing Itself.*
>
> Ernest Holmes
> *The Science of Mind* (23)

The beauty of this process is that we live in a spiritual Universe of pure intelligence, perfect life, dominated by love and reason, and the power to create. It may seem confusing because we are individually subject to the effects of race consciousness (humanity's consciousness) to the extent that we buy into it. As our personality unfolds, we can consciously create our desires on the outer with the use of inner thought. Our conclusions and assumptions thus become part of the relative cause of our outer experience. By learning and practicing this teaching, we bring higher levels of understanding and truth into our consciousness, which lawfully out-pictures in our experience. This concept can be understood intellectually, but the greatest experience in life is to use it, thus the gift of becoming a Science of Mind Practitioner.

The medical profession doesn't have the ability to heal the soul. It is primarily focused on healing the effect, the physical problem, with little concern for the original cause. Billions of dollars are spent each year destroying diseased tissue, removing growths and unwanted things in the body. In time, more of this energy will be focused on the real cause, the mental cause that lies behind all unhealthy conditions. As people search for answers to the visible cruelty and hardships in the world, a renewed effort has surfaced that searches for answers on the spiritual path. Subconsciously all people seek to return to unity with God. It is inherent in our nature.

Spiritual healing is based in rediscovering truth, being in touch with the wholeness of the Universe. It is finding inner peace, that special contact with God that is always there, but may be temporarily hidden from view. It is possible to feel the presence and power of God and through that peace, find harmony—in the body, relationships, work, and prosperity. Since the Presence is always there, grace and joy unfold in life only in proportion to our recognition and acceptance of It. It is useless to sit back and wait for God to make Its presence known. That work is up to us.

The unconscious feeling that there is good available to each one of us and we ought to have it, is permanently part of the makeup of human beings, according to the teachings of Emma Curtis Hopkins, a famous spiritual healer in the late 1800s. She believed this feeling lived within every human being and provided a tremendous source of strength. To her, the word "good" had a special meaning—the search for good is actually a search for God (Miller 3). In her work, she taught students the value of telling the truth about their good so it would appear in their life. She recommended being truthful about what we want, putting away any and all ideas that could interfere with it.

Meister Eckhart, a thirteenth century German mystic, felt God's image is like a living spring underground and although it vanishes from our sight, it remains alive and as our consciousness blossoms, it is like removing the soil, and we see it again (O'Neal 95).

Goodness and unity are keys to this one undivided spiritual system that never expresses itself in fragments. Parts of God are not literally scattered about the Universe. If the Universe is perceived as divided, the belief in duality will mentally create the illusion of separateness from the Source. This separation manifests in undesirable ways, and perfectly reflects and expresses the Law of Cause and Effect. An Effect always mirrors Cause, the image of our consciousness: an impersonal, neutral, receptive, and reactive law. It is a mechanical principle like any other. If we are dishonest in life, dishonest people may show up in our life. If we are not truthful, people may lie to us. If we are confused, we will end up in confusing situations. The law operates irrespective of personal opinions. But when we turn back to oneness through Spiritual Mind Treatment, we are again aligned with the power of God, the power of good, and the attributes of light, love, life, peace, power, beauty, and joy.

There is disillusionment along the spiritual path for many people, because all of a sudden some find out that

» This is it. God is not going to come and save us, because God is all there is and is already everywhere present.
» Change is continuous and the less we get upset about it, the easier it is.
» The purpose of the game of life is to play the game.

Is the work difficult? Not if the divine grace of God is allowed to operate through us, as us. It is possible to effort and worry every step of the way, but if we let go and allow the nature of the Universe to be our guide, life will unfold sweetly and more beautifully than anything that could have been anticipated. When the rush of everyday life obstructs our good, it is Spiritual Mind Treatment that shifts consciousness and brings us back into unity with the Source. Therein lies its power.

Growth is an endless force in all that occurs and, like a magnet, pulls all people toward God with no conclusion or final revelation. At all times the Law of the Universe pulls us toward the recognition that God is in everything. Meister Eckhart wrote that God is not just the good things in life, because all of life is God (O'Neal 9). At times progress on the path to a higher consciousness can seem very slow, but there are no limits except the ones we place on it. These principles are in operation at all times, and the outer demonstrations in life clearly show our level of understanding. We are all IT—the express manifestation of the infinity of God, and individually we have the opportunity in this lifetime to discover it.

Now, we must open up the doors of our conscious-
ness and expand and expand and expand, and no
longer think in the terms of the backyard lot but
in the terms of the infinite nature, in the terms of
the universe.

Ernest Holmes
Love and Law (15)

Religious Science understands human misery to be the result of ignorance of the Law of the Universe. It is awareness of our divine nature that frees us from ignorance and all its effects. Anything that helps in this pursuit of knowledge, to overcome suffering without negatively impacting others, is good. The purpose of the Science of Mind philosophy is to teach the nature of reality, make it personal to everyone, and then to use this power for good for definite and specific purposes. Making use of the law to change our life experience and perceive the ever-presence of God is the only reason for studying it.

The key to the whole thing—that, just as Einstein
says, energy and mass are equal, identical, and inter-
changeable, which means they are the same thing.

Ernest Holmes
Anatomy of Healing Prayer (112)

Therefore, it is Intelligence that moves, since that is all there is. The Intelligence of God has created all and it operates on the principle of law and order. Why? We will never know. How? It can never be fully explained. It just is the way it works. Using affirmative prayer, called Spiritual Mind Treatment, the Universe receives our thought and creatively acts upon it. The effectiveness of a treatment depends on the clear thinking, logical affirmation or arguments, and realization of the Practitioner in establishing First Cause.

It is wishful thinking to imagine being able to do a treatment and eliminate all the problems in life. The experiences of life seem to be in confrontation with and divert attention from our true nature, undermining inner peace or destabilizing health or relationships. If these effects are not given power, they will not have any power. There is only one power in the Universe, and the Science of Mind Practitioner works constantly to stay in that knowing. To the degree one knows and accepts the truth, is the degree to which treatment will succeed. The Practitioner looks at disease, sickness, or any other form of ignorance, confidently knowing it has no power. Nothing prevents the principles of a God-centered Universe from manifestation except our recognition of it. It is Truth that sets the Practitioner and the client free.

> *What I really want to know about are the results*
> *of your beliefs. Are you satisfied with the results?*
> *Where are you going in life?*
>
> Ernest Holmes
> *Science of Mind* (xxi)

The Practitioner is a teacher of Truth and offers an understanding of this Truth to clients so they may recognize their own divinity and turn from having faith *in* God into having the faith *of* God. As a teacher, the Practitioner carries a light into a darkened room; through treatment, truth is revealed. In this way, the room and the mind of the client will then remain illumined.

C h a p t e r   2

T H E   C O N C E P T   O F
S P I R I T U A L   M I N D   H E A L I N G

⟪⟪⟪

Omniscience:

God possesses knowledge necessary to create anything.

Omnipotence:

a Power before which a seemingly intractable condition
is nothing.

Omnipresence:

this Power everywhere present.

Frederick Bailes
Healing the Incurable (24, 27, 28)

We live in a Universe of pure intelligence, perfect life, dominated by love and reason and the power to create. As we evolve,
it is our own conscious cooperation with the Laws of the Universe
that move us forward. Every form of matter is Spirit and the
intelligence of the Universe is in the essence of every one of its
manifestations, regardless of form. The individual intelligence in
each person is able to use this truth to fully express itself in terms
of freedom.

The Laws of the Universe are always in operation, but seem hidden much of the time, and we operate in general ignorance of them. It is being conscious of our life experiences, both positive and negative, that lends insight into these laws. We can tap the benefits of the laws we come to understand, knowing that they are not personal, but universal. Doubting the operation of Universal Law eradicates its benefits.

Spiritual Mind Treatment is the art and science of inducing thought within the mind of the one doing the treatment, which perceives the life of the client as a Divine, Spiritual, perfect idea. Spiritual Mind Treatment is affirmative prayer, spoken in a scientific manner and in faith. It is a statement placed into the Law, embodying the concrete idea of our desires and accompanied by an unqualified faith that the Law works for us, as we work with it. Prayer or treatment is the alignment of our individual thought with the perfect right action of God.

Treatment is not something one does to another, nor to a situation. It is always the thing one does for oneself. Treatment is an action in thought alone. It opens up avenues in the mind, expands consciousness, and lets reality through. Spiritual Mind Treatment involves deliberately inducing constructive thought within the medium of Universal Mind, which in its creative function as Law tends to produce in the outer world an equivalent of our inner thought. It is an art, a skill that can be learned and taught. It is an act, something that is done, and is not done until you do it. It is a science, a technique that operates in accordance with definite Law.

Five Steps in Spiritual Mind Treatment

1) RECOGNITION

God is the source of all, the unlimited power.

GOD IS...

(Declare your definition of God in many ways.)

2) UNIFICATION

God acts through me, as me, in me and all life.

I AM...

(Declare your spiritual nature, the reality of all people in many ways.)

3) DECLARATION

I initiate my life experiences through my thought. I now choose my desired experiences.

I ACCEPT...

(Declare the truth about the person in the here and now. Go from the general to the specific. Deny each symptom and affirm the Truth for each.)

4) THANKSGIVING

I joyfully accept the now present activity of Law acting through my intention perfectly.

I GIVE THANKS...

(Declare the work is already done.)

5) RELEASE

I release any doubts or concerns as I let go and let God, "the Father within," do the work. I now feel and act as if it were so.

(Declare a strong statement of love and truth, releasing it to the Law.)

AND SO IT IS!

Spiritual Mind Treatment is not faith healing or a "get rich quick" scheme. It recognizes that God is all knowing (omniscient), all powerful (omnipotent), and everywhere present (omnipresent). Energy and mass are equal, identical, and interchangeable, therefore treatment is effective when we know that God responds, God will always be there, and God is within. This is the perfect expression of unity. There is no difference between the mind and what the mind does. Truth cannot be confined to a definite space and time. Treatment or affirmative prayer is technically a nonlocal event, not confined to a specific moment or place. It operates outside the present, in the infinity of space and time. It doesn't go anywhere, but is present simultaneously everywhere. As Thomas Troward explained, Universal Intelligence is everywhere and there is a corresponding responsiveness hidden in each person's nature ready to be called upon (*Edinburgh Lectures* 14).

> *As subjective mind it must reproduce exactly the conception of itself which the objective mind of the individual, acting through his own subjective mind, impresses upon it; and at the same time, as creative mind, it builds up external facts in correspondence with this conception.*

Thomas Troward
Edinburgh Lectures (49)

Dr. Craig Carter referred to it this way: "All have said: *it is done unto you according to your belief!* And the changing of your belief is entirely within your own control" (*Power of Mind* 5). Therefore, the atmosphere in our mind is critical to how we feel and experience life.

When Jesus talked about how to pray, he said to believe you have what you want and you will receive (John 16:24). It is the nature of the Universe to give us what we are able to take, at the level of our ability to receive. It cannot give us more; it has already given all. If we don't experience it, we have not yet fully accepted the greater gift. Each individual state of consciousness taps the same source, but each person has a different level of receptivity, thus the multiplicity we see throughout the world.

Health is defined as a condition of wholeness or freedom from defect or separation. To heal is to make whole or bring back together that which has been separated. It is a process of taking the client to an honest place of self-discovery so that recovery will last, and conscious spiritual growth can continue. Healing is uncovering and erasing false images and thoughts that we have accumulated, letting the true perfection of the Universe reflect in our conscious mind. As we rush toward God, God rushes toward us with the Universal power of good.

> *Treatment opens up the avenues of thought, expands the consciousness, and lets Reality through; it clarifies the mentality, removes the obstruction of thought and lets in the Light; it removes doubt and fear, in the realization of the Presence of Spirit, and is necessary while we are confronted by obstructions or obstacles.*
>
> Ernest Holmes
> *Prayer* (39)

The value of being a Practitioner is the gift of seeing perfection, knowing there is nothing to heal, only something to reveal. The value for the client is that the Practitioner's belief in Spirit is greater than the client's belief in the necessity of undesirable conditions.

> *If you believe there is nothing you can do about what you are and how you live—then you are absolutely right.*
>
> Dr. Tom Costa
> *Life!* (142)

Unpleasant and undesirable conditions cannot remain unless there is a person/body/spirit present to create and experience them. The purpose of Spiritual Mind Treatment is to determine First Cause, the true issue from beyond the perceived problem, and then to effect change in the consciousness of the one doing the treatment, so that the undesirable condition will disappear. How fast can this happen? To the degree that the Practitioner accepts Spiritual Truth, it is instantaneous in its demonstration. The process of healing is the time, effort, and depth the Practitioner undergoes in the realization of Truth. **True healing is healing the cause that produced the effect.**

Psychic healing may produce a change in effect, but won't change cause, leaving it to produce other effects. Why does it work this way? The greatest minds do not know. Like any law, we just accept what is known about how it works. In the view of Ralph Waldo Emerson, our power is within ourselves, as well as the authority to use it. He felt not only do we have a God-given right to independent thought and action, we have an obligation to exercise it (33). "A foolish consistency is the hobgoblin of little minds" (41).

A treatment session with a client is not about change, it is about realization. It is misleading to tell clients that through treatment they can have whatever they want. Theoretically this is true, but it is frustrating for most people since the result may not take the form they expect or anticipate. In truth they CAN HAVE whatever they CAN ACCEPT. This is why so much of the work is assisting the clients to recognize their divinity. If Practitioners believe that their work is with the ego, that in itself is a belief in duality. The work is to recognize one's divinity and oneness with God; to raise the veil of consciousness, which keeps us from recognizing and accepting our own perfection.

> *We are not depending upon chance but upon the Law.*
> *The responsibility of setting the Law in motion*
> *is ours, but the responsibility of making It work*
> *is inherent in its own nature.*
>
> Ernest Holmes
> *Science of Mind* (305)

Part of the spiritual process is to keep redefining the ego and the goal of life. Ego desires that we get life organized, then stay put so the rest of life is easy. Ego debates what it would cost to demonstrate or get something. The result can be a great arrogance if the person ends up working only with ego and law, but without God. When we get to the point where we are not infatuated with "things," we have found the secret.

It is Universal-consciousness that enables healing to take place. It is the conviction in the Practitioner's mind that the client is completely perfect and whole. Evil has no power in itself and cannot be perpetuated in the face of truth. The negative effects are a result of a misunderstanding of truth. If we focus on the effect—the sickness or disease—it remains as it is. Nothing can be done to heal the condition until we recognize it as an illusion, a veil that has covered the true nature of God manifest as this person.

> *It is through the medium of this greater mind, this broader field of spiritual realization, that practitioners work; calling upon the deeper side of life upon that Universal Medium which unites all people and all events into one unitary wholeness.*

> Ernest Holmes
> *Can We Talk to God?* (95)

Chapter 3
OPENING THE HEART

Did you know that the word heart appears over a thousand times in the Bible? Although the word *heart* is commonly associated with love as in "Valentine heart," and courage as in "brave heart," and grief as in "broken heart," in the Bible the word *heart* is a metaphor for the self.

Deuteronomy 10:12 . . . Serve the Lord your God with all your heart.

Proverbs 23:26. . . . . Trust in the Lord with all your heart.

Matthew 6:21 . . . Where your treasure is, there your heart will be also.

Marcus Borg's book, *The Heart of Christianity* (151), explains that the Bible has many metaphors about the human experience that show both a predicament and a solution:

In bondage, we need liberation.

If we are estranged, we need to reconnect.

If we are blind, we need to see.

If we're in the dark, we need enlightenment.

If we're hungry, we need food.

And if our heart is closed, it needs to be opened.

There is an emerging pattern that is transforming religion in the United States today. It is opening the heart through experiencing oneness with God, with Spirit.

In all spiritual traditions, a closed heart is one that has turned away from God and feels proud, puffed up and hard. Borg writes about many of the symptoms that show up in people with a closed heart, such as:

» limited vision and hearing, because they do not see or hear clearly;

» self-deception, because they believe their own thoughts;

» bondage, because they want only what the hard heart desires;

» bitterness, because they lack gratitude;

» ordinary, because they are insensitive to the wonder and awe around them;

» lost, because they have lost track of the mystery around themselves;

» exiled, because they are preoccupied with themselves and separate from others;

» hardened, because they are not open to the feelings of others; and

» self-centered, because they are insensitive to injustice.

(*Heart of Christianity* 151-154)

We probably all have experienced one or more of these symptoms, but the good news is, Marcus Borg tells us, the closed heart is the natural result of the process of growing up. Well, if our heart is feeling closed, how do we open it? Borg says *we* don't do it, the Spirit of God does, and the Spirit of God operates in thin places (*Heart of Christianity* 154). He reminds us that God is the one in whom we live and move and have our being. We actually live in a two-dimensional reality.

There is the world of our ordinary experience, like reading this book in a place where we feel the temperature of the air and hear sounds around us; then there's the sacred Spirit, a "thin place," where we become aware of the sacredness all around us, where we experience God shining through everything. A thin place is where the ordinary meets the extraordinary. A thin place is where the veil momentarily lifts, and we see the essence of Spirit alive all around us. Thin places are where our hearts open.

In some Centers and other New Thought churches, it is common to ignore rituals and the trappings of traditional religion: no statues, no crosses, no coming up front to be saved. Yet a Personal Blossoming ceremony at Easter and candlelighting at Christmas are thin places where we bring our intention and our attention together to open our hearts. As students, our daily invitation is to create unique opportunities and experiences—and third year classes for practitioner training offers those opportunities.

Chapter 4

THE PROFESSIONAL PRACTITIONER

A Practitioner is a person who is trained in the art, science, and skill of Spiritual Mind Treatment. Licensed to practice professionally, a Practitioner is bound by a high code of ethics to respect a client's confidences, and is dedicated to the cause of helping others. Going inside, a Practitioner gets clear about a client and his desire to change, so that the One Mind in which we all live and move and have our being, will work positively in the client's life.

Practitioners are unique individuals and do not "look" any particular way. Typically they love life and are curious about it. In *The Power of Decision,* Dr. Raymond Charles Barker wrote, "We are the means by which earth becomes heaven" (129). We were not created to be average. Our life experience is self-made. This talent, unique to each of us, is to be used successfully or unsuccessfully—that is our decision. Immanuel Kant, an eighteenth century philosopher, taught that we lift ourselves up and out of ordinary experiences by raising our minds to extraordinary ideas and then learn how to put them into practice. He believed there were three great questions in life that wise people seek to answer: What can I know? What ought I to do? What may I hope? (308). This is the path of a Practitioner.

By using Spiritual Mind Treatment, a Practitioner demonstrates principle. **Learning how to align with Spirit and demonstrate principle comes only from personal experience.** No one can teach this. We cannot have a corresponding realization for a client beyond the level of realization within ourselves. That is why Jesus said that if the blind lead the blind, they will both fall into a ditch (Matthew 15:14).

> *Scientific mental practice begins and ends in the consciousness of the one giving a treatment.*
>
> Ernest Holmes
> *How to Use Science of Mind* (33)

The purpose of being a Practitioner is to deepen one's own consciousness and connection with God. A Practitioner must have a strong commitment to "go to God" and serve others. This longing helps the Practitioner to do clear treatment work and in truth know that *the longing for God is God*. This allows inspiration to pull us through spiritual practices versus allowing desperation to push us.

We never try to sell this philosophy. It is only by our use of it, how we live and act, that people will become interested in knowing more about it. In meeting with clients, a Practitioner presents the Science of Mind teaching to them and lets them decide if they want to accept it. Therefore, the Practitioner is also a role model. The people we meet at centers and those who come as clients desire to activate their own potential and are looking to the Practitioner for help in changing something in life. The job of the Practitioner is to present to the world one more honest mind with a loving heart that lives a productive life.

As our interest grows in becoming a Practitioner, we recognize it means living by the golden rule of justice and fairness. Practicing unconditional love will open our heart and increase intuitiveness. Foresight and wisdom will keep alive qualities that stimulate growth. When we come to see things in a state of joy and deep gratitude, all perceptions of limitation fade away.

Peace of mind cannot be found in the past or the future, only in the present. Our peace of mind adds to the consciousness of peace for our clients and throughout humanity. Each day should start on an inner basis, free of stress, full of health and peace of mind. During the day we are conscious of how we contribute to others who have lost their peace of mind. We live a life of humility; we are humble, respectful, cooperative, peaceful, and never arrogant. This means perceiving and cooperating with the positive desires of other people. We see and feel a need and, if possible, fill it in an appropriate manner.

When we are willing to meet the needs of others, our own needs are met. Again, the Law of Cause and Effect rules. Reading about the life of Albert Schweitzer may lend more insight to this idea. He founded and operated a hospital in Africa, devoting his life to healing others. He found the kind of freedom we all want through fearlessly pursuing his instincts, by rising above a life of struggle to do what truly pleased his soul. His philosophy was based on one vital concept: reverence for life.

The consciousness of Truth alone is the tool of a Spiritual Mind Practitioner. Three important qualities for spiritual mind healing are persistence, flexibility, and patience, which creates space for clients to progress at their own level of acceptance. We cannot guarantee a client specific results in terms of effect, but we can guarantee that shifting cause or establishing a new cause will create a new effect—*cause* meaning the sum total of all beliefs and attitudes. The result of treatment is unpredictable, so we are treating to know that the client allows his subconscious mind to reflect a deeper understanding of spiritual ideas.

Practitioners do not see themselves as healers any more than mathematicians assume they are the principle of mathematics—yet both are trained in how to use principles. When doing treatment, the Practitioner knows that truth is superior to the condition that is to be changed. This belief in ultimate goodness must be greater than any apparent manifestation of its opposite.

Being a Practitioner doesn't mean we are without our own problems or effects. The mark of a Practitioner is that we first take responsibility for our life, and then learn how to use treatment to address what needs to be changed within us. When we have a personal challenge, we go back to the Declaration of Principles and figure out where we got off track and bring ourselves back to center. A Practitioner maintains the highest behavior under all circumstances. Many people believe in darkness, so it is the Practitioner's job to reveal light. To be successful in spiritual mind healing, we take time to see ourselves in unity with the client, not separate from him. If there is a feeling of separation, it is our mind that needs healing. A Practitioner is consistent, not different with different people, and is committed to be honest and truthful with everyone.

Clients are often afraid of choosing a new direction or option for their life. When people say they don't know what to choose, actually they want the Practitioner to choose. Choosing for them does not work. We can facilitate their choice through general suggestions, but not specifics. The best part of a session is when the client makes her own choice. Treat that the client knows the right thing to do. The art is to help her see and implement her own highest cause.

At one time or another, the Universe pushes everyone to a limit where they wonder what is really going on in life. Sometimes crisis is the only reason people look to the spiritual path for an answer; otherwise they may not. A Practitioner helps people recognize they are at the gate, the gate of choice, where they can step into a world of greater good. The more clearly clients see this, the easier it is for them to step through the gate. This is the beauty and joy of being a Practitioner.

Integrity

Since the Law always puts the Practitioner's word into motion, we must have confidence in our own power. Our word must not be compromised with contradictory signals that could create a negative reaction within the Law since life is always corresponding to our inner spiritual state.

To be successful, a Practitioner maintains the highest level of integrity: holding our life in line with our moral code based on principle. When we act in accord with our true higher self, our actions, words, and thoughts express it. Integrity requires being honest with ourselves most of all. That is why daily spiritual practices are so important—going to that quiet space within where we confront ourselves, what we are really doing, and how we are living. Our life is what we have made it. It is a reflection of our inner self. Any sense of discomfort with what we are experiencing in life should be looked at in relation to integrity. A Practitioner cannot wear a blindfold and pretend everything is all right when it is not.

We are challenged to live in principle again and again throughout our lives. To the degree we recognize how far in or out of integrity we are with principle, is the degree our life expresses harmony. It requires awareness at all times. By maintaining a life of integrity, not only do we empower ourselves, but we empower everyone around us.

Values

Personal beliefs about what is most important, our belief in right and wrong, good and bad, are values, and they impact every aspect of our life. Over time many values become unconscious and instinctively guide our actions and reactions. When we feel out of sync or in turmoil, we can often trace it back to being out of integrity with our basic value system. Instead of letting this incongruity operate at the subconscious level, Practitioners should periodically reassess both their primary values and value hierarchy. Values change and if our present behaviors don't match our values, it is time to modify one or the other to resolve the conflict.

Values are specific and emotionally charged, such as when to tell the truth, whether to give a full day's work for a full day's pay, how important it is to be on time for an appointment, whether or not we would cheat on a test, etc. Often values are formed in childhood and are based on the environment we lived in and the role of our teachers and parents. When we become adults, those values don't always serve our needs and should occasionally be evaluated. Values are motivating factors in life, so being out of integrity with values can drain our enthusiasm for things we love to do. There is nothing worse than having strong values tugging at us from opposite directions.

Periodically we should reflect on the highest values we hold in life. What are the top ten? What values do we hold about relationships, commitments, love, the place we work, the type of work we do, our role as a parent, the health of our body, ways to have fun, methods of creative expression, the amount of money we make, etc.? Does our life reflect living in integrity with these values? If not, we should change our actions or change our values, but we must get back in integrity and regain inner harmony.

A brief overview of the requirements of Licensed Practitioners follows. For detailed information, see the Centers for Spiritual Living "Policy and Procedures Manual," Chapter 8.3.

Typical Requirements for Practitioners

1) Maintaining membership in an affiliated Member Community and permission of the Senior Minister.

2) Successfully completing Practitioner Training as established in the CSL Education Code (Section 10.3).

3) Satisfactorily passing the written licensing exam and oral panel.

4) Completion of all documentation and payment of fees.

Activities a church may ask of Practitioners:

» Teach classes
» Treat daily for the ministers
» Treat daily for the licensing organization
» Attend an occasional evening service or lecture
» Hold seminars for church members on how to do treatment
» Help with a ministry of healing, doing treatments on request
» Teach an occasional class on The Essence of Religious Science
» Assist at Sunday services
» Lead volunteer or Seva teams (*Seva* is the Sanskrit word for selfless service.)

License Renewal for Practitioners

1) Reassess and recommit to a life of spiritual service.
2) Abide at all times by the Code of Ethics and Policies and Procedures.
3) Be an active, loyal, and supporting member of a Member Community.
4) Perform the required number of hours in service as a Practitioner.
5) Engage in a minimum of forty (40) hours of appropriate educational activities and class work during each two (2) year licensing period.
6) Complete the license renewal process and pay all renewal fees.

What Practitioners Do Daily

1) Support our personal growth through spiritual practices in order to maintain a conscious spiritual awareness for ourselves, our center, and others

2) Support the center through Seva in volunteer activities and service

3) Support individuals who seek our help so that they may recognize cause(s) at work that may be creating limitation or opportunities to implement cause for new growth, success, new opportunities, etc.

   a) Teach the principles of Religious Science
   b) Teach people how to do their own treatment
   c) Know the truth for people
   d) Express love, support, compassion and caring in a personal way

Chapter 5

RENEWING OUR HEART

The process of personal transformation, or being born again, is the center of our spiritual life. It often feels like a death and resurrection. It feels like dying to an old way of living and being born into a new way of being.

In the synoptic gospels of Matthew, Mark, and Luke, the path of death and resurrection is the way they believed Jesus taught. In Matthew 16:24, Jesus said, "If any man will come after me, let him deny himself, and take up his cross, and follow me." In Luke 14:27, Jesus said, "And whosoever doth not bear his cross, and come after me, cannot be my disciple." In John 9:25, there is the story of the blind man, his sight restored, throwing off his cloak and following Jesus. *Once I was blind and now I see.* That is personal transformation.

Think about it. At some point after birth we begin to be self-conscious, self-aware; we begin to experience the separated self. This is the story of Adam and Eve and the central message of the Garden of Eden. Living in a perfect state, they became conscious of opposites, of good and evil. They fell for a belief in separation and were expelled from paradise. This is the birth of the separated self, an experience that cannot be avoided. We cannot develop into mature human beings without self-consciousness, yet it puts us in the experience of being self-centered. As we grow up, we learn a language with labels and categories that divide our world. We get parental messages, cultural messages, and, if we're lucky, some of us get religious messages. Our individual identity is formed and it shapes the way we see the world. From there we are filled with messages that drive us to a quest for appearance, achievement, and affluence. Are we attractive enough? Are we cool? Do we have enough money? These are all lures that take us away from that spiritual innocence. If we go too far to achieve these things, we find ourselves in a trap and our fall into exile is very deep.

When we find ourselves outside the Garden of Eden, we take on the characteristics of being preoccupied, prideful, miserable, and insensitive. We are blind and can't see. To be born again, spiritually, is to return from a separation from God. To be born again means we begin to live our lives from the inside out rather than from the outside in. We let the false self die and let the real person inside be born. The deeper we fall, the more challenging it is to get our heads above water again.

Sometimes we are called to be born again on a daily basis. During the course of a day, we begin to feel like we are carrying a burden and get out of sorts from something we read or hear. At that moment we have forgotten God. When we remind ourselves of our divine creation and that of everyone around us, we feel lighter . . . we come back from the darkness.

In Judaism it is called "the way." In Islam it is "surrender." In Buddhism it is "letting go." For Religious Science, it is called personal spiritual transformation—(PST) Pssst! When you're feeling that need to be "born again," Pssst! It's like baking a cake. You've got to have the right ingredients. To be born again as a Religious Scientist you need three things: one cup of awareness, one cup of intention, and one cup of practice.

Awareness is becoming conscious of our relationship with God. God is in relationship with us all the time. Spirituality is about our getting back into a relationship that already exists. It's about letting go of the fears and coming back to the party, like the prodigal son that regained his awareness and came home. If you're running from a dragon, it's time to wake up and be aware that in Religious Science, we believe we create our own monsters. The first two steps in Spiritual Mind Treatment, affirmative prayer, are about coming into the awareness of our divine heritage.

The second ingredient is intention. What intention do you have for your relationship with God? Mother Teresa said, "I'm a little pencil in the hand of a writing God, who is sending a love letter to the world" (Vardey 116). That is total surrender. But life is so busy, there is so much to do. The Chinese written character for the word *busy* is a combination of two other characters: *killing* and *heart*. How is being so busy working for you? There are two kinds of busyness, the kind that is empowering and, as Alan Cohen puts it, the busyness that sucks (163). Killing . . . heart. And then you will be pushed to be born again. Not a good way to go. So ask yourself about your intention, how much time will you spend being so busy *killing heart* vs. how much time you will spend embracing the beauty of life and your relationship with God?

The third ingredient is practice. Pssst! Our spirituality is flexible enough that we can be born again on a daily basis, if needed. Renewing ourselves is the heart of a spiritual life. This is what coming together with like-minded people at a center is all about. The center is like a midwife, here to help you through this process of being born again. We believe we are born of the grace and the spirit of God, and this grace is full of hope—hope for a new beginning. None of us are the same as we were yesterday—it's the way of the Universe, the upward spiral of the Universe.

Chapter 6
THE RELATIONSHIP OF HEALING

The most important step a client can take in resolving a problem is to request the assistance of a Practitioner. The moment she takes that step, the path of healing begins. Know at this point, the client is open to hearing the truth, and at the client meeting, she will receive what she needs.

The Practitioner inquires about the Effect in the client's life that she would like to change, and then works to identify the Cause. The Law of Cause and Effect says we reap what we sow, what we contemplate we become. As Dr. Michael Beckwith says, our "energy goes where our attention flows" *(Life Lift-Off Cards).* The explanation the client gives of the Effect will indicate where to begin looking for the error in belief, which is Cause. If life is not working on the outer, there is a misunderstanding on the inner that is not as visible as the effect.

The fact that an effect is present is proof that cause exists. The Practitioner does not hold the discussion on effect for very long, since focusing only on effect could keep the client talking in an endless circle with no resolution. The inquiry should dig through the layers, going deeper and deeper to root out cause. We don't stop until we get there. The ego doesn't want to look at cause and will put up defenses, but as we burrow in, going from the head to the heart, the dam breaks and cause is revealed. Often it is when clients stop talking from their intellect and begin to feel uncomfortable that emotions finally surface. We don't let them stray from this effort. We inquire, listen, and teach.

Jesus taught that a mental attitude of faith arrived at through love can perform miracles. When the disciples of Jesus asked how to pray, he told them to shut out any doubt, go within and make a request, believing they possess the object of their desire, and disregard all appearances to the contrary. "Therefore I say to you, whatever things you ask when you pray, believe that you will receive them, and you will have them" (Mark 11:24). We know this as the Law of Cause and Effect.

At a Practitioner Workshop at the Asilomar Conference Center in 2003, Dr. Carolyn McKeown-Fish described what she called the LITT Process:

Listen .... *with a desire to help the client*

Inquire ... *to discover what they really want.*

Teach ..... *them to be their own master, teaching principle when appropriate*

Treatment

At times it might help to ask clients about their understanding and vision of God. Some people believe in an angry or vengeful God, while others believe in a loving or maybe distant God. It may help to reunite the client with a God who may have been distant and get back in touch with the unconditional love God represents.

Thomas Troward cautioned about seeing ourselves as an individual personality that ends where another person begins. (*Edinburgh Lectures* 67). This is separation and is a misunderstanding of principle. The Practitioner and the client are not separate in truth, so the Practitioner creates the opportunity for the client to open up and remain in a conscious state of receptivity. This is important so that the client feels comfortable admitting his belief, and the Practitioner is open to offering the truth. With the barriers removed, the Laws of Nature take over. When a barrier is broken, a vacuum appears, which means the client is open. Now the love and truth offered by the Practitioner can flow in. Eric Butterworth explains it this way in *The Universe Is Calling:* "God's will for us is so intense, so continuous, that it even filters through our willfully closed mind" (42).

It is our job as Practitioners to focus on the nature of the client's life as Spirit, which God has made manifest in total perfection. The work is to be an instrument through which God-realization occurs. We do not sit in judgment of a client or resolve the effect that has shown up in his life. There is **no** advice to give and **no** purpose in suggesting to a client a right or wrong way to do something. If the Practitioner gets caught up in anxiety, it only perpetuates secondary cause. We just open up and let the power of God do the work. If a Practitioner gets caught up in the drama of the client's effect, it may cause the client to be concerned about the Practitioner's abilities.

There is never a session with a client that is unsuccessful. We cannot be responsible for completely new effects in the client's life, because we do not know his level of acceptance, his receptivity to the concepts of truth. The client has a right to express life the way he feels is best for him, whether we perceive it good or bad. Trust is the key to the success of a Practitioner. Know that our time with a client is working itself out in its own way since there is nothing in the Universe that could work against it.

During the inquiry phase of the client meeting, know that the connection between cause and effect is present. Say only what you see—and not what you think the client should do. Suggest that she look at choices and think about what could be the highest path. The Law of Cause and Effect says that if she changes one thing in her life, her whole environment changes. Change or moving beyond the problem may feel uncomfortable for the client if it requires leaving thoughts, people, or places behind.

Holding our meeting in a place that helps facilitate and support the client can make the shift much easier. Spiritually there is no reason for anyone to stay in a negative environment. It is a choice. As all metaphysicians know, suffering is not virtuous.

If we do a treatment over the telephone, let the client know that after the treatment, we will hang up right away so that we don't diminish the release in the treatment by continued talking. When doing the treatment in person, we don't hang out with the client after the treatment; otherwise the subject is likely to come up again. We let the treatment sit with the client so she can hold it in her consciousness.

Payment for Services

The work of a Practitioner is a licensed professional service. Recommended fees for our service have been established by the licensing organizations, but the services of a Practitioner are never withheld because of an inability to pay. It is customary that some form of compensation be given either at the time of treatment or in the future.

If the payment is a problem for a client, spend some time discussing prosperity and the Law. Financial success is one way Spirit expresses. Limitation, even in the area of money, indicates some error in thinking. Life is a perfect mirror reflecting our thoughts, which include thoughts about prosperity. Since there is no lack in God, there is no need for lack in our lives. We are surrounded by Infinite Intelligence and can demonstrate monetary supply through right thinking.

Many people lament that they have to spend their days making money in order to meet their financial needs, and feel that their spiritual life must be compromised due to the time required at work. Many people also feel that God could not possibly be involved in the financial affairs of daily life. This attitude only succeeds in cutting a person off from the potential of serving God through work and earning money.

The great saints know that God is in everything. Behind the myriad forms and guises of this world, the saints see only the unchanging Spirit, manifesting this infinite drama. Paramahansa Yogananda said, "Making money honestly and industriously to serve God's work is the next greatest art after the art of realizing God" (*Where There Is Light* 72).

Confidentiality

In the search for Cause, the Practitioner expects the client to be totally open, honest, and willing to go deep enough to find the answer. This requires the client to be vulnerable, which may bring up irrational fear. Meeting with the client in a place that feels safe, quiet, and relaxing, where the client feels unconditional love and understanding from the Practitioner is very important. Being entrusted with the deepest thoughts of a client requires mutual respect. Honesty and integrity define the relationship, and confidentiality is its cornerstone.

There are unspoken expectations of confidentiality that must always be honored. Recognizing the client's right to privacy ensures she can share her most intimate thoughts and fears with us. The Practitioner must also maintain a high level of integrity to be worthy of the client's trust.

Counseling vs. Interviewing

It is the nature of humanity to help relieve suffering and pain. Our choice in the practice of Spiritual Mind Treatment must always be focused on the unity of the client with his true nature. If we stray and see the effects in a client's life as separate from his true nature, our tendency may be to try and "fix" the effect. This creates a sense of separation, a duality where a Practitioner could buy into the suffering. This can hold the client in the effect of limitation, dependency, and helplessness.

During the interview, the Practitioner seeks to understand the effect that the client wants to change. From this point, the Practitioner turns away from the effect and works to locate the cause, the error in belief that has made itself manifest. If the Practitioner gets caught up in fixing the effect, it becomes a slippery slope into confusion. Ram Dass recognizes this compulsive reaction to fix the effect in a client's life as a "toxic tension" that can perpetuate the client's suffering. He explains that this naturally compassionate part of our heart can get mixed up in a struggle between love and fear and show itself in misguided ways (*How Can I Help?* 63). We have all experienced pity, professional warmth, or compulsive "fix it" behavior in others as they resist getting involved in an unpleasant situation. None of this is helpful to the client.

> *To help those in need is indeed a great privilege,*
> *but the blind cannot lead the blind.*
>
> Ernest Holmes
> *Science of Mind* (415)

By slipping into fixing the effect, a Practitioner unconsciously forces the client to become a patient. If the Practitioner gives advice on how to work with the effect, personal opinion can set in, blinding both him and the client to the Truth. This is unfortunate because it ignores the cause, leaving it to continue manifesting problems. Working only on effect helps the client hold on to the problem she wants to get rid of. This approach is far from being compassionate, because it maintains a sense of duality. When a Practitioner recognizes that he is caught up in the effect of a client, it is time to stop and immediately do a treatment for clarity.

> *What the healer does is to mentally uncover and*
> *reveal the Truth of Being, which is that God is in*
> *and through every person, and that this Indwell-*
> *ing Presence is already Perfect. We separate the*
> *belief from the believer and reveal that which needs*
> *no healing.*
>
> Ernest Holmes
> *Science of Mind* (418)

Legal ramifications are another reason a Practitioner should avoid attempting to fix the effect. A counselor and a client establish a legal, professional relationship that makes malpractice law applicable. Although ordained ministers have typically remained exempt from malpractice liability because counseling is a function of their ministry, the Practitioner is neither a minister nor licensed counselor. Legally a counselor is required to both "exercise reasonable care" in practice and possess a minimum level of "special knowledge and ability." Malpractice liability exists when it can be proven that 1) a counselor owed a legal duty to her client, 2) the counselor breached that duty by failing to meet the requisite standard of care, 3) the client suffered some demonstrable and compensable harm, and 4) that harm was caused by the counselor's breach of duty (*Professional Malpractice*.http://www.legalmatch.com/law-library/article/professional-malpractice.html).

Malpractice law requires that counseling be given without harm or detriment to the client. A breach of standard care by a counselor is the determination of whether the counselor's instructions were suggestions or prescriptions for change. For spiritual as well as legal reasons, it is in the best interest of the Practitioner and the client to avoid the area of fixing an effect.

Chapter 7

PRACTICAL FORGIVENESS

A recent article I read about forgiveness said one of the most fundamental laws of the universe is that everything seeks to perpetuate itself. *Perpetuate* means to try to cause something to last indefinitely. Now that may seem an odd way to think about the subject of forgiveness, but follow this thinking . . . if you watch any of the nature shows, you see that a species perpetuates itself by defending itself, and eating other animals or plants, and producing offspring. As human beings we survive by defending ourselves, by eating other animals or plants, and producing offspring. Yet, as a thinking and reasoning animal, we also perpetuate our belief of right and wrong, good and bad, in the way we handle the tasks of obtaining food, shelter, and clothing. We get really comfortable with our belief system and like to surround ourselves with people who share our beliefs. From there we like to perpetuate our opinions on every subject, personality, and experience, and we are always very glad to find someone who shares our opinion.

Another belief we perpetuate is how we deserve to be treated. When someone treats us in a way that seems less than what we believe appropriate, our ego jumps in to protect us. Usually this means we instantly make a judgment about the other person. If this person treats us badly again, our judgment gets a little stronger, until our drive to defend ourselves is so strong that we can actually want the other person to pay for his transgression. Have you ever felt that way? When someone does something we don't agree with and then something bad happens to him, there's that righteous feeling. For some cultures in the world, the drive to perpetuate beliefs and right the wrongs against them creates such anger and resentment that it drives people to kill each other. This drive happens on a large scale in the world and a small scale in our daily life.

As Practitioners, we notice that people are pretty consistent. Those who study human nature say we form our basic set of values and beliefs between the ages of ten and twelve years old. After that, we respond pretty consistently to events and experiences throughout life, until we have a significant emotional event. A significant emotional event causes us to reevaluate our beliefs about what we are doing, how we are living, and our beliefs about what is right and wrong, good and bad. Basically our attitude about how to live is perpetuated until something shakes us to the depths of our soul. For a lot of us, this happens when we go through a divorce, which is one of those traumatic times when everything we believe is questioned.

We don't have to wait for a significant emotional event to bring more joy and happiness into our life. We can stop perpetuating any patterns of negative opinions, judgments, and emotions, and wake up to the words of the world's greatest mystics and teachers and use simple forgiveness. As Religious Scientists, we believe that our shortcomings will be forgiven to the precise degree that we forgive the shortcomings of others. How did Jesus say it? He told Peter to forgive not seven times, but seventy times seven (Matthew 18:22). Forgive a lot! As the Lord's Prayer says, "Forgive us our trespasses as we forgive those who trespass against us." There is no qualifier here.

Possibly the reason true forgiveness is so difficult is that it is seen as unjustified. It feels like if we forgive, we are overlooking a really bad thing that happened. There are many examples of horribly evil leaders throughout history, tyrants and dictators who butchered millions. Should we perpetuate hatred for them? No. Should we forgive them? Most definitely! Harboring anger, hatred, even disgust about people we have no contact with, only poisons us. Historians who study the atrocities of history report that these events are mass phenomena that include even the most decent people who, on their own, would never even think about doing such awful things to other human beings. Every person who takes part in these horrible things is always there by right of his own consciousness. No one person is to blame. If you study these events, it is healthy to ponder whether in the same circumstance we would have acted any differently. It is a mysterious question.

And when we read about those who were harmed by these evil ones, we often find that they have forgiven those who harmed them, or at least put their bitterness aside in order to get on with their lives. Viktor Frankl and Nelson Mandela come to mind. Once they were out of bondage, they didn't waste a lot of time harboring grudges or perpetuating hate. They accepted what was, forgave those involved, returned to a place of inner peace, then worked to awaken the world to greater peace and understanding.

Jesus said, "Why beholdest thou the mote that is in thy brother's eye, but considerest not the beam that is in thine own eye?" (Matthew 7:3) It's that darn ego again that wants the widest latitude for ourselves, while refusing to grant any to others. That is why forgiveness is the ultimate act of generosity to ourselves. It is the ultimate act of freedom, since it liberates us from our bondage to past hurts or losses.

As Religious Scientists, we believe in the Law of Cause and Effect. What we give, we receive. We are in control of whether we perpetuate more peace in our life, or more hurt, jealousy, anger. We know good begets good and evil begets evil. Yet, our ego wants to exonerate itself at all costs, frequently by casting blame on someone else. The article I was reading said the ego minimizes our shortcomings while exaggerating those of others, so forgiveness is not so much a spiritual act as it is an art, a way of compensating for our own distortions of reality. Refusing to forgive perpetuates conflict and suffering. As human beings with an ego, we can expect to have moments when we are so good, we are disgustingly good—and moments when we say or do something that hurts others. We each have the capacity to bring goodness or pain into the world, into our families, and into our communities.

Practical forgiveness is the willingness to forgive someone while we are still angry. We're so angry we're burning ourselves up inside. Practical forgiveness requires an inner detachment; it is a refusal to feel abused any longer. What did Jesus say on the cross? "Father forgive them for they know not what they do" (Luke 23:34), which is a good statement to perpetuate in our mind when we feel offended. The purpose of forgiveness is to remove our own suffering and reestablish ourselves in wholeness.

The goal of forgiveness is to change ourselves so a greater demonstration of harmony is manifest. That is the reasoning behind the commandment to love thy neighbor as thyself. It is through love, not judgment, that we will find greater peace in life.

If someone in our life is a real problem, one question is, do we love that person? Until we love him or her, the problem won't change. It will just take a different form. The Law of Cause and Effect is alive and well. We can perpetuate a belief that the problem has nothing to do with us until we are reminded that everything that happens in our life is our doing. Using simple forgiveness, we can forgive the person and he may not change, but *our* life changes for the better. The purpose of forgiveness is to remove our suffering and reestablish wholeness. Liberation is ours with practical forgiveness.

Chapter 8

MENTAL PROCESSES IN PERSONAL HEALING

It is very challenging to work with a client without a face-to-face meeting. If the client is serious about clearing up a difficulty, a personal meeting is always preferable since much of what a client communicates is nonverbal. During the initial contact, explain how a treatment session works: first we'll have a discussion about the problem, then some questions in order to identify the cause, and finally a spiritual mind treatment at the conclusion. Be sure the client understands the cost (the published fee by Licensed Practitioners). This information helps the client relax and view the Practitioner as a professional. We offer a valuable service.

Client meetings should be held in a safe and quiet place, such as a center, to ensure minimal distractions. A home may be fine if there is a place where the client will feel comfortable, preferably in a spot specifically designated for this work. If a client does not want to meet, probe to find out how serious he is in resolving the conflict. It may be that he is in a crisis situation and needs help immediately. Others may just want you to "do a treatment" or possibly some sort of magic, while they do nothing.

It is important to have an answering machine so that a client can get a response in a reasonable time. Prompt answering of calls is a priority, but at the same time, we must be practical—only emergencies need top priority. If our schedule does not fit with the needs of the client, recommend another Practitioner and make the arrangements to minimize the hassle for the client.

As a professional, we may have to tell a client what she doesn't want to hear. This may create pain, but it is unavoidable. See the client through the pain, allowing her to recognize the level of suffering bottled up inside. This is true compassion and true serving, and why it is so important that the meeting environment feels safe and comfortable.

If a client is focused on someone else in his life that is in trouble, such as relative or a friend, the Practitioner helps the client release that loved one to her highest good. While it is not appropriate to do treatment for a third party without her request or permission, we can treat for the client regarding his realization about a third party.

Process

We sit in close proximity to the client, from three to five feet away, and keep tissues easily within reach. It is never necessary to touch the client. We ask why he has come and then watch and listen. So often, a client will do to the Practitioner exactly what he is doing in his life that has created the problem. We ask him to pause at times and clarify what we have heard, using statements like, "What I hear you saying is . . ." If he is rambling and we don't hear any logical connections, we ask again why he is there and what exactly he wants out of the meeting.

We direct the process and if a client has a control issue, he may try to take control of the session. We pay close attention since everything we do with a client is part of the process. Can we identify the mechanism he uses, his control drama?

Health Problems

Working with a client with health problems or who is under medication can sometimes be challenging. Here are a few ideas for those with special needs:

» If a client is taking medication, continuing to take medication is her choice, and when a doctor sees improvement, the client can make the choice whether to stop the medication.
» Assure the client that going to a physician doesn't invalidate or conflict with spiritual mind treatment.
» If the client is perceived to be ill and doesn't want to see a doctor, discuss the possibility that she may be in denial.
» Do not validate a choice made by the client regarding a doctor. The manifestation of healing may actually be found in the relationship she has with medical professionals.
» Doing treatment for a client who is sick is okay. Both perfect health and sickness are true, yet incompatible. Do treatment knowing that physical healing is one way to demonstrate the power of treatment. In truth, we do not know what success looks like in the bigger picture.

Always remember, a healing that demonstrates can be measured. It is not the place of a Practitioner to give a client medical advice, or any type of advice. The goal, the appearance of the goal, and the seeker are one.

Death and Dying

Our belief is that God is changeless, yet the form that God takes is always changing. It is expressed as unity that exists in the midst of diversity. Death is just another experience, a higher order of change. Whereas we are comfortable with slow change, the sudden death of a loved one may make it very difficult for a client to reconcile, release, and let go.

In truth, we died somewhere in order to be born here. Birth and death are the same thing when we recognize the multitude of ways God expresses, and being human is just one of them. When a client has a close friend or loved one who is dying, or if he is dealing with the prospects of his own death, reactions may vary. Overall, people work through fairly predictable stages of emotion in order to cope with the situation. These include denial, isolation, anger, bargaining, depression, and finally, acceptance. In her book *On Death and Dying*, Elisabeth Kubler-Ross shares that throughout all these stages, there is one constant factor that enables the person to keep moving through the process, and that is hope (122-138).

In *The Tibetan Book of Living and Dying*, Sogyal Rinpoche shares that the two spiritual things we can do for the dying are give them hope and help them find forgiveness (212). Guilt, regret, and depression can overwhelm a dying person. A Practitioner can focus instead on his accomplishments, his virtues, to find peace of mind.

Ernest Holmes taught, "The will of that which is Infinite can never be finite" (*Science of Mind* 269). He believed that the will of God cannot be death, because God is the Principle of Life and could not produce death without destroying Itself. "Death has nothing to do with life everlasting, and is but an impatient gesture of the soul, wishing to rid itself of a body no longer useful" (*Science of Mind* 478).

After the experience of physical death, we carry with us a complete subjective memory that links our experiences as we express through our consciousness. Therefore, we are the result of what has been before. Why is this? We will never know. All that is important is that we are here in this life to express through the use of our body and mind. As we go from one experience to another through this life and the next, however it is expressed, we are continually carried forward. "God is not the God of the dead, but of the living" (Matthew 22:32).

As a Practitioner, we may be working with a client who associates death with something bad and frightening, or as punishment. Denial of the truth about death allows the client to avoid facing the reality of his own death. The way to help clients who are afraid of death is to explain through principle the importance of living while they are here. The purpose of life is self-discovery. "All that means anything is that while we live, WE LIVE, and wherever we go from here we shall keep on living" (Holmes, *Science of Mind* 270).

Chapter 9

SPIRITUAL WARRIOR TRAINING

It is quite common to find that what draws new people to our centers is a desire to deal with personal pain. There is something inside that urges us forward to resolve pain, and experience more love. It is as natural as the sun rising in the morning that our spiritual nature urges us forward to break through the pain—to do more, be more, give more, and love more. Thomas Troward explained the upward spiral of the Universe, the natural force of the Universe that impels us to continue to evolve, which is why when we put on the brakes in our life or create obstacles to growth, we experience pain (*Edinburgh Lectures* 10).

Ernest Holmes had one key message—there is a power for good in the Universe and you can use it (*Science of Mind* xxiii). Like anything worth achieving, spiritual growth takes training . . . spiritual training. At times life may appear as an army of problems coming at us. Becoming a spiritual fighter is battling for good, for truth and justice in our own home, at work, or in our community. Although we may not resolve things by being a spiritual fighter, the journey through life creates the spiritual warrior. A warrior has fought the battles and rises to a level where he sees a better way. One day we become one with the love of the universe, and we have become a spiritual warrior, a warrior of love. Until then, we are all in training.

Rumor has it that Abe Lincoln said if he had six hours to cut down a tree, he'd spend the first five hours sharpening the ax. The work needed to become a spiritual warrior does take tremendous energy if our ax isn't sharp. In Religious Science, we sharpen our axe by recognizing there is a divine urge in each of us, pushing us to learn and grow. It is our personal evolution. Ernest Holmes taught that spiritual wisdom starts the day that we know from now on, every discovery is either a discovery of the self or related to the self in the Cosmic Mind (*Science of Mind* 416). The self must raise the self by the self.

Some people search for a teacher in the quest to understand life. Some look in the mysterious East, only to learn that the answer to the quest comes perhaps while visiting relatives. Our evolutionary journey may seem a bit like being in Disney World's Tower of Terror, a high speed elevator ride where the doors open erratically on random floors. Riders hold on tightly as the doors fling open onto different views of the world. The opposite experience would be climbing the steps in a ten-story building with the floors grouped this way:

Floors	1-2-3:	Basic Self
	4-5-6:	Conscious Self
	7:	Higher Self

On this journey, we basically walk in to the first floor, then when we are ready, we climb to the next floor. We climb, turn on the light, deal with our issues, clear them up or don't clear them up, then at some point, we get enough energy to start climbing again. It takes energy to climb, and sometimes we give up for a while, or we find ourselves falling down the stairs.

The First Floor is Survival: isolation, fear. Our thinking is childlike and we operate on instinct. When we need to act, fear can paralyze us, which is dangerous. Fear contracts our energy and attracts the things we fear. It isn't people or situations that contain fear; it just bubbles up at times if we haven't mastered it yet. Think about the millions of people in the world that are dealing with life at a basic survival level.

The Second Floor is Creativity, where there is sexual energy, people engaging in pleasure of every kind. Energy amplifies everything—our mind is brighter, emotional power intensifies. But energy has to be used. Whenever there are internal obstructions, excess energy becomes destructive. Anger grows into rage, sorrow into despair, a concern becomes an obsession, and physical pain becomes agony. The body will do what it must to use up excess energy. If it isn't spent consciously, in creative ways, it will still get used, but not in a positive way. Pain is the Basic Self's last resort in getting us to wake up and grow.

The Third Floor is Power, a world of order, balance and beauty. Here we gain personal power over the Basic Self and desire of the ego, but the challenges are self-discipline, clear intentions, duty, integrity, responsibility, focus, commitment. The third floor is the arena of the battle. It is cluttered with issues of discipline and self-restraint. It might be called the finishing school for the Basic Self.

For many, just to climb these three floors in a lifetime is a great achievement. It is when we take the great leap to the fourth floor that we consciously come in contact with our higher self. The growth spurts continue, but by maintaining our path of spiritual training, the recovery time gets shorter and more pleasant to experience.

How can there be world peace when millions are stuck on the first floor, dying of starvation? How can there be world peace when millions live a life of hate, rage, anger—-the terrorist bombings? How can there be world peace when millions are stuck in pure self-gratification and narcissism—leaders driven by the quest for power and greed? In Religious Science, we find a high percentage of people who have moved on to higher levels of consciousness, and we believe that ultimately, conscious evolution will bring all people to the highest level of evolutionary growth, but not necessarily in this lifetime.

There are always those people who think there is a short cut. It is natural to want to experience the upper floors without mastering the first three. Often we try to distract ourselves from the dilemmas of daily life. Many well-intentioned, lonely, desperate people try to generate spiritual experiences through a variety of techniques. They want to cut to the head of the line. But if they aren't grounded, if they haven't built a solid foundation, they soon fall back and have to start all over again. Maybe you've heard the saying, I spent a lot of time climbing the ladder of success only to find out it was leaning against the wrong wall.

As Practitioners, we meet with people who feel a loss of purpose or emptiness, who are questioning the purpose of even being alive. I always ask if they do any volunteer work, what we call Seva, selfless service to God. It is daily life that is the training arena on the spiritual path. As Jesus taught, whoever would be the greatest among you is the servant of all (Matthew 23:11). Service is the most honorable path to walk on our evolutionary journey. We can move beyond the three basic levels of life by serving others, not out of self-interest or guilt or social conscience, but because there's nothing else we'd rather do than open our heart to all of God's divine creation.

When we serve others, we no longer have to practice the way, because we become the way. We meet the higher self by becoming the higher self. It is a process that cannot be forced. Holmes wrote that the aim of evolution is to produce people who, at the objective point of their own self-determination, may completely manifest the inner life of the Spirit (*Science of Mind* 471). Evolution is an effect of Intelligence, not its cause. Evolution can only follow involution, growth from within.

It is important to embrace all three selves: Basic Self, Conscious Self, and Higher Self. The Basic Self is not to be ignored. We need to master the basics to give us roots, a strong foundation. Any issues we have in the area of basic training need to be cleared up in order to take the Great Leap between the third and fourth floor.

The most profound tool for change and spiritual growth is practitioner training. It is the greatest investment we can make on the path. As part of a spiritual community, this gift of life is a great journey we share together, for we are all on the spiritual path together.

Chapter 10

BEGIN WITH THE PRESENT

A Practitioner listens to the client's story about the negative effects in her life, knowing in Truth, it is just a shadow. The effect we see is a mirror or mental equivalent of its cause. In *The Power of Decision* Dr. Raymond Charles Barker writes that it is not the sun that causes the shadow (effect), it is an object, person or obstruction (misunderstanding of the Law) that causes the shadow (9). When the obstruction is removed, the sun shines once again. The sun was there all the time; it never went away.

When clients see only a shadow, their back is toward their true nature; God's reality is not alive in their experience. Living in a shadow creates doubt and confusion, which may be what a client is exhibiting. A rule of thumb is that clients will do to the Practitioner what they are doing to themselves, i.e., being indecisive, argumentative, avoiding, blaming, denying, etc. When we are grounded in truth, we see the client's story as only a shadow, no matter how ugly it may appear. If we are not feeling grounded, we can easily get sucked into the story and all of a sudden feel indecisive and argumentative, avoiding the hard topics. Dedication to daily spiritual practices, as well as a treatment for clarity just before a meeting, helps guard against getting caught in the drama of the client. In Science of Mind, we speak to the adult, not the inner child. If we are in doubt that we are speaking with the adult personality of a client, clarify it with him.

The pain and suffering experienced by the client can be seen as a wakeup call from God. The degree of pain involved may be the only thing that finally pushed the client to call us. The Practitioner has no judgment about the effects in a client's life. There is no reason to look down upon any soul's approach to God. Jesus said, "Do not judge according to appearance, but judge with righteous judgment" (John 7:24). In other words, do not be confused by the conditions around us.

Karma is not fate—it is a consequence of cause and effect. For every action, there is an equal and opposite reaction. Our fate is not sealed. Change the cause and the effect will cease to exist. Thoughts and feelings are also effects. Cause can be changed up to the moment before effect. The Universe is flexible; it is we who hold tight to cause and effect. A Practitioner needs to know the specifics of a problem—a general statement will not do. Neither will the client's conclusion of cause. Question your clients about what is specifically happening in their life, including the actual names of people. This helps to bring feelings to the surface about the events they are experiencing.

Ideas for Identification of Effect

» What does the client want?
» Ask for specific examples of the effect.
» Ask how he would prefer it to be.

» Use active listening: "I hear you saying . . ."
» Pursue the emotional points—what is it about?
» When we feel off track, ask the client again why he called you.
» If the client goes off on a tangent, ask what it has to do with the problem.
» Identify false images and beliefs.
» When we hear a race consciousness statement—stop the client and ask where it came from and then identify it as a purely limiting idea. **Teach principles.**
» Restate truths.
» Show the client how his choices were based on false truths.
» Repudiate any statement of lack, evil or limitation.
» Stop and explore any "Ahas."
» Paint a linear picture to recap the process of how wrong belief resulted in bad effects, and how the Law will respond positively to a new cause or belief.

It may be appropriate to use empathy with clients, sharing from our own experiences. If their problem was previously our problem, they might find comfort in knowing how we solved it and other ways it might have been solved. Be blunt and say what feels necessary.

It is okay to say the issue is something we have had to work on, so the client knows we connect with it, but we DO NOT indicate that we currently have the same problem; otherwise the meeting becomes two people with problems and no answer between them.

> *Problems are indications that something creative must be done in mind.*
>
> Dr. Raymond Charles Barker
> *The Power of Decision* (71)

Time spent arguing with a client is a waste of energy. When someone is argumentative, we don't buy into it and instead do treatment to know there is no resistance. Take everyone right where they are and build on the affirmative thoughts they already have. Employ their faith in the most simple and direct manner possible. Gradually point out that their faith in other things is built on the same principle we are using—that of nonresistance. Resistance is a lack of understanding.

After listening to negative statements from a client, the Practitioner is the first one who has to be healed. The entire sense of lack, evil, and limitation must be repudiated. As always, Practitioners deal with their consciousness and not with the consciousness of the client. There may be indications that the client feels overwhelmed if she says things like "I can't do it all." This shows a belief in duality and a disconnection from the Source. In truth, know there is never too much to handle, and the world is always in balance. Now is the time to release personal responsibility, which also works for the Practitioner. Our duty is to do the work and release the outcome to the highest good.

Time is also an effect, so we don't get caught up if the client's problem is not enough time. Time can be used as a limitation, when in truth there is no time. The Universe, Spirit is timeless. Ernest Holmes teaches that God is not limited by any form, and this includes time (*Science of Mind* 317). This concept is reinforced by physicists such as Helmut Schmidt of the Mind Science Foundation, whose article "Can an Effect Precede Its Cause?" was published in the prestigious journal *Foundations of Physics* (463-480) in 1978. He concluded, "Apparently, present mental 'efforts' were able to influence past events about which 'Nature had not yet made up her mind.'" Dr. Larry Dossey, in his book

Healing Words, says "The nonlocal view [of prayer] suggests that the mind cannot be limited to specific points in space (brains or bodies) or in time (the present moment), but is infinite in space and time; thus the mind is omnipresent, eternal, and immortal" (84).

When the client hits an "Aha!"—a revelation—stop and let her explore it. If she starts repeating "Yeah, but . . ." be sure to stop and explore those areas for errors in belief. "Yeah, but" indicates the client is not ready to take what the Practitioner has to offer. If the client says "I don't know," "probably," or "maybe," know that somewhere in mind the client does know.

Money is a reflection of how people feel about their life and their acceptance of limitations. Do they feel rich in life, free to be prosperous? If they feel abundant and free from worry about money, they have the mental equivalent of a healthy mind. There are many common beliefs about money: there is not enough; too much causes pain and suffering; it is the root of evil; it is usually obtained dishonestly. If these ideas come up, they should be explored and the error in belief corrected.

Chapter 11
WALKING THE RAZOR'S EDGE

Walking the razor's edge . . . sounds risky doesn't it? As Religious Scientists, we know that the razor's edge is that place where we exist, right here, right now. It is the very instant between the past and the future, what is called the everlasting now.

Often we get anxious for the future in a good way, like planning to see a famous play, or if we're single we may get anxious about a hot date we've got scheduled this weekend. If we're anxious about the future because we think it's going to be difficult, like a court appearance or a funeral service, an election or a war, all this anxiety, both good and bad, keeps us out of the present moment where we are creating that future. If we're anxious about the future or what happened in the past, we're either on one side or the other of the razor's edge. When we carry around guilt about something that happened in the past or have regrets that we didn't do this or that, or if we're focused on how good our life used to be and regret that it's not that good now, we're focused on the other side of the razor's edge.

In Religious Science, we believe our future manifests from what we're thinking and believing now, the actions we take now. Our conscious mind puts into our subconscious mind desires and feelings that bring together those energies that create our future. When we're focused on the past or the future and ignore the present moment, what will we get? I call it potluck, whatever just happens to show up. In *The Science of Mind*, Holmes says it this way: "Mind must be directed or it will do nothing of permanent worth" (396). *Permanent worth*. He further says, "Our mental acceptances should be filled with conviction, warmth, color and imagination. The creative power responds to feeling more quickly than to any other mental attitude" (398).

And finally, "We should be careful to distinguish day dreaming and wistful wishing from really dynamic and creative treatment. When we treat we do not wish, we KNOW. We do not dream, we STATE, We do not hope, we ACCEPT. We do not pray, we ANNOUNCE. We do not expect something is going to happen, we BELIEVE THAT IT HAS ALREADY HAPPENED" (399). The better we get at walking the razor's edge, anxiety dissipates, fear diminishes, and anger disappears.

In this past century there have been two leaders, who through great trials and tribulations, walked the razor's edge. They saw the past and knew what the future could be and stayed on the path, doing what they could do, one day at a time. They trusted in the process of nonviolence, knowing it would bring about better conditions. For Mahatma Gandhi, it was better living conditions for the people of India and independence from Britain. For Martin Luther King Jr., it was better racial relations. For our individual lives, our goals may be to improve our relationships, our work, or our lives. We can learn a lot by studying the lives of these two men in how they worked to achieve their goals.

Taking a lesson from Gandhi, King taught five points about nonviolence to help people understand it would bring about a better world:

1) King cautioned that this is not a method for cowards. People using nonviolence for change are not passive. Although they are just not physically aggressive, their mind and emotions are always active, strongly active spiritually. They are non-aggressive physically but dynamically aggressive spiritually.

2) Non-violent resistance does not seek to defeat or humiliate others, but to win their friendship and understanding.

3) Non-violent resistance is directed against the forces of evil rather than against people who are caught up in those forces. In 1957 MLK said to the people of Montgomery, Alabama, "The tension in this city is not between white people and Negro people. The tension is between justice and injustice, between the forces of light and the forces of darkness" (*Testament* 8).

4) Non-violent resistance avoids not only external physical violence, but also internal violence of spirit. At the center of nonviolence stands the principle of love.

5) Non-violence is based on the conviction that the universe is on the side of justice.

(*Christian Century Journal* 158-167)

There are two important facts: First, the line of progress is never straight. For a period, a movement may follow a straight line, and then it encounters obstacles and the path bends. It is like curving around a mountain when we are approaching a city. Often it feels as though we are moving backward and we lose sight of our goal, but in fact we are moving ahead, and soon we will see the city again, closer.

Second, final victory is an accumulation of many short-term encounters. To lightly dismiss a success because it does not usher in a complete order of justice is to fail to comprehend the process of achieving a full victory. It underestimates the value of confrontation and dissolves the confidence born of a partial victory by which new efforts are powered. Martin Luther King Jr. called on people to create the American Dream, a land where people of all races, all nationalities, and all creeds can live together as brothers and sisters. The substance of the dream is expressed in these words: "We hold these truths to be self-evident, that all men are created equal, that they are endowed by their Creator with certain unalienable rights, that among these are life, liberty, and the pursuit of happiness." This is the dream (*Testament* 208).

King said that in order to make the American dream a reality, we must develop a world perspective if we are to survive. The American dream will not become a reality devoid of the larger dream of a world of brotherhood and peace and good will. The world in which we live is a world of geographical oneness, and we are challenged now to make it spiritually one. To do this, we must get rid of two strange illusions. First is the myth of time, popular to those who say that we must wait: "If we just wait and be patient, over time things will work out." But social progress never happens when we just sit and wait. It happens through the tireless effort and the persistent work of dedicated individuals (*Testament* 213).

The other myth is thinking that we can solve a problem either through legislation or by education. But it is not a question of either/or; change requires both. Religion and education will change attitudes and legislation controls behavior. It may be true that the law can't make a man love me, but it can keep him from lynching me . . . and I think that's pretty important. In Religious Science we say all is love and all is law. Love points the way, and Law makes the way possible.

In his famous 1965 speech, "The American Dream," King said that nonviolent resistance is one of the most magnificent expressions in the world. In less than a year lunch counters had been integrated in more than 142 cities in the Deep South, and it was done without a single court suit. It was done without spending millions of dollars. And even if nonviolent resistance does not bring about immediate results, it is constantly working on the conscience, using moral means to bring about moral ends (*Testament* 214).

The most well-known and most quoted speech by Dr. King was "I Have a Dream," delivered in front of the Lincoln Memorial on August 28, 1963, during a civil rights march on Washington. In that speech he said,

> *In the process of gaining our rightful place, we must*
>
> *not be guilty of wrongful deeds. Let us not seek to*
>
> *satisfy our thirst for freedom by drinking from the*
>
> *cup of bitterness and hatred. We must forever*
>
> *conduct our struggle on the high plane of dignity*
>
> *and discipline. We must not allow our creative protest*
>
> *to degenerate into physical violence. Again and again*
>
> *we must rise to the majestic heights of meeting*
>
> *physical force with soul force.*
>
> (*Testament* 218)

As practitioners, we learn to free ourselves from whatever bondage we perceive. We do what we can to find that place in the here and now, where there are no regrets about the past or fear or anxiety about the future. We know that with God all things are possible. With our creative mind and connection with Universal mind, all things are possible. Then we, too, are free at last.

· ⇢⟩⟩⟩ ·

Chapter 12

LOOKING FOR CAUSE

· ⟨⟨⟨⇠ ·

By the time a client has contacted a Practitioner, the cause creating a negative effect in his life can be very difficult to see quickly. Emotions distort the client's' ability to logically think through to the solution even when the client is another Practitioner. Often his opinion is that if only the world, situations, people, or conditions changed, he would be just fine. Seldom does he recognize that the change must be made within.

> *You are the result of your past decisions. You will*
> *become and experience the result of your present*
> *decisions.*
>
> Dr. Raymond Charles Barker
The Power of Decision (22)

Whatever has caused the effect for the client, feel assured that it is a misunderstanding of truth, of reality. Thomas Troward explained that all positive conditions result from the active presence of a certain cause, while all negative conditions result from the absence of such a cause. He said conditions, whether positive or negative, become causes in their own right and produce new conditions *ad infinitum*. Conditions are not causes in themselves, but links of a chain that keep reflecting our beliefs. Effect will always equal its cause (*Edinburgh Lectures* 56).

CAUSE			Various Results
M I N D	→	**Visible action** →	**and**
SPIRIT			**Future Possibilities**

The first step in identifying cause is recognizing that there is no room for blame in spiritual healing. The client has experienced the effect for reasons we may never comprehend, for a purpose on the soul or universal level that may be greater than we can imagine. The only weapon that can effectively be used to change cause and thus change effect, in every case is truth—the awareness of God. When this contact with God occurs, grace flows and healing can occur. Delving into a client's past doesn't guarantee her future will be any better. All neuroses are caused by attempting to avoid legitimate pain.

> *We may not be able to see very far, but there is one safe general principle to be gained from what has already been said about causes and conditions, which is that the whole sequence always partakes of the same character as the initial cause.*
>
> Thomas Troward
> *Edinburgh Lectures* (77)

We are all subject to race consciousness, which is a thought pattern that automatically operates in everyone. It bombards us in the media, and through contacts with people. It is embedded in what we are taught and is absorbed by members of society unless it is consciously rejected. Race consciousness is not an individual cause, but can be found at such an acceptance level, it becomes a choice. This can often be the case when a client is frustrated in achieving success. There is no need to fear that God wouldn't support us in success, if in reaching out for our greater good, we let go of something else. Instead, race consciousness says it is best to be mediocre and not stand out from the crowd.

When the client gets emotional, ask what it is about, for we are getting close to Cause. Emotional outbursts such as crying are one way to know the client has touched that part that seeks to be healed. Stop and investigate what is causing the emotion, because we are almost there.

Persistent problems and patterns stem from behavior that was originally intended to help the client overcome a problem. It worked so well in other areas, it was repeated and eventually became a habit, a subconscious process. When the client realizes this, he may think it will be a difficult pattern to quit. Remind him it doesn't take long to establish a new groove in consciousness. Treatment will cut a new groove, a new road, so the old one will be gone. When the ego believes things are being taken away, it is actually God shifting things around. Know for your client that the future holds more power, love, happiness, and satisfied relationships (which are all inner states). It is all available, but up until now it just hasn't shown itself in physical form.

All is love—the impelling force; and all is law—the execution of love. Remind clients that just doing affirmations won't solve a problem. It must be full acceptance of the nature of the Universe. There is never a time when we are not moving toward God. It is the essence of nature never to be satisfied; so the business of life, the constant progression of life, is always evolving and is never finished.

Identifying Cause

In my experience, the life experience the client describes for seeking treatment seldom shines light on the root cause. It takes inquiry to find and clarify the cause, which shows up as a thread in a client's life. For example

a) A client asks for treatment to heal back pain.
b) Upon inquiry, you find out she has back pain because she is worried about her son who has chronic pain from an accident and is dealing with it by abusing prescription drugs.
c) Upon further inquiry, you find the thread of cause and effect. She asked for treatment to heal back pain. She is worried about her son who has chronic pain from an accident and is dealing with it by abusing prescription drugs, and finally, the son is living with her and verbally intimidating and abusing her.

After discussion, cause is determined to be unworthiness, which showed up as feeling inadequate as a mother, the inability to draw boundaries with her son, seeing the son that she raised as less than an adequate human being, which she feels must be her fault, and therefore she is deserving of abuse.

Another example

a) A client asks for treatment to heal her relationship with her husband.
b) Upon inquiry, you find the issue with the relationship is that her husband tells her he hates their life together, verbally abuses her, and ignores their children.

c) Upon further inquiry, you find the thread of cause and effect. She asked for treatment to heal her relationship with her husband who tells her he hates their life together, verbally abuses her, and ignores their children, and finally, the client's mental anguish is because he is unhappy that she doesn't cook meals and does not keep a neat and tidy house.

After discussion, cause is determined to be guilt, which showed up as the client feeling inadequate as a wife since she did not cook or clean the house; and her disregard for her husband's needs and feelings, apathy for the needs of the family, and an unwillingness to even try to work as a team.

Identifying the Cause of Health Problems

Health is normal and sickness is abnormal. All things respond to mind, including health. Merely hoping to regain health is a delusion; it carries no authority because there is no serious emotional impact in hope. A person seeking health must *decide* to be well before any spiritual therapy can start producing results. The expectation of being well is the key. There are many people who cannot be helped or healed through mental means, because they will not take the responsibility of making their own decision for health. The maintenance of health takes determination.

Although there are no foolproof examples of possible links between cause (the subconscious belief the client is holding) and health (how it expresses in his life), some patterns have a tendency to be related, such as

Hate: abscess, goiter

Anger: bad breath, burns, fever, infections, sprains

Fear: addictions, anemia, apathy, excessive or loss

	of appetite, belching, body odor, cholesterol, crying, diarrhea, far- and nearsightedness, frigidity, headaches, heartburn, indigestion, influenza, nervousness, ulcers, stomach problems
Pride:	gallstones, knee problems
Burden:	shoulder pain

The Practitioner does not make a judgment about the health of a client. It is not known whether it is a good or bad experience for the client to have ill health, nor do we know enough about the big picture to be able to judge, compare, or classify a physical condition. The Practitioner does not know the life's work of the client and whether perfect health would help him achieve that spiritual goal. The focus of healing is always on the mind in order to have a lasting effect, not on the form.

After a considerable amount of time, if identifying Cause seems illusive, explain to the client what has been observed at that point. Ask what he would specifically like treatment for and focus on that. It is not necessary to determine why the effect has manifested. The treatment will still be effective because changing the cause changes the results in one way or another. Let the client know that after the meeting, if things become clearer, there is always an opportunity to come back for another session. If he would like the Practitioner to be informed on how the treatment unfolds, that contact is made only by the client, not the Practitioner.

Chapter 13
CREATING A POWER TREATMENT

When creating a spiritual mind treatment, it is wise to put as much thought, feeling, and emotion into stating the Truth as one did in describing the problem. As we speak our word, feel the exhilaration in every cell. We feel the warmth, the release of energy, the joy, the feeling of healing. As Ernest Holmes advised, we should feel as though the whole power of the universe is running through the words we speak.

Power Words

Power words can enhance our thoughts and feelings. There is a difference in the energy of saying, "I am healthy" versus "I am a vibrant expression of the love of Infinite Intelligence that created me as the perfect expression of health." Here are some power words that can enhance the energy in your treatments:

Accelerate	Action	Active
Alert	Best	Capable
Certain	Clear	Compelling

Conceive	Confidence	Convenient
Creative	Dependable	Determine
Discipline	Discover	Dream
Dynamic	Effective	Efficiency
Energy	Easy	Energetic
Enthusiastic	Establish	Excel
Excellence	Expand	Free
Freedom	Fun	Grandeur
Greater	Guaranteed	Healthy
Ideal	Improve	Independent
Infinite	Initiate	Innovate
Light	Listen	Love
Magnificence	Motivated	New
Original	Perform	Powerful
Precise	Proceed	Proficient
Progress	Proven	Pure
Quick	Release	Reliable
Responsible	Results	Right
Safe	Secure	Simplify
Solve	Stimulate	Streamline
Strengthen	Strong	Success
Systematic	Thorough	True
Undisturbed	Unleashed	Unlimited
Vital	Wisdom	Yes

The best healer is the one who sees nothing to heal, who sees only Reality, only the Divine, only the Truth.

H. B. Jeffery
Principles of Healing (157)

Four Ps

In his book *Five Steps to Freedom*, Dr. John Waterhouse describes the four elements to making Step Three, the Realization step of spiritual mind treatment, most effective (49). In addition, he suggests we use words that are most meaningful for ourselves that are Personal, Present, Positive, and Precise.

1. Make it *Personal* to our lives.
2. Know it works in the *Present* moment.
3. Focus on the *Positive*.
4. Be *Precise* in stating the truth.

Invoking Principle

After a while, we may find our words dealing with principle getting a little stale. Typically we use, "God is all there is," and "I am one with God," but there are more ways to reinforce and reflect on the Truth. For instance

» A law manifests the mental equivalent we hold in mind.
» A person is a center of God Consciousness.
» All Cause is mental.
» All conditions manifest from a mental cause.
» All life is sustained and supported by the Self-Givingness of God.
» All that God is, I am.
» All that is visible has its cause in the invisible.
» All things are possible with faith.
» Anything mind thinks it can un-think.

- As we give love, we attract love in return.
- Body is thought in form.
- Distortion of a Spiritual Principle is a mental cause of illness.
- Divine Mind is infinite and inexhaustible.
- Every condition responds to mental action.
- Expectancy speeds progress.
- God can do for us only that which God can do through us.
- God does not know illness or disharmony.
- God doesn't judge.
- God gives unconditionally, gives to all and to all alike.
- God is All, in All, as All.
- God is my Source.
- God is the only power there is.
- God is the supportive power in every situation.
- God is your unlimited source.
- God only sees perfection.
- God's life can never be diminished, and God's life is the only life there is.
- Human life is the expression of individual consciousness.
- I am in the right place at the right time with everything I need.
- I am One with God.
- In God all things are possible.
- In God there is only balance.
- In God there is only wholeness.
- It is done to you as you believe.
- It is the nature of God to seek ever greater Self-expression.
- Life is eternal.
- Life is ever evolving.
- Life will be to you what you are to it.
- Love eliminates anything unlike itself.

» Money is an energy of which there is always enough.
» Money is an extension of who we are.
» Money is God in action.
» Nothing happens by chance or circumstance.
» Only mind creates.
» Only you, the individual, can limit your success.
» Opposing thoughts cancel each other in the Law.
» Our bodies are pure spiritual substance.
» Our bodies are self-healing entities.
» Our experience of life is a reflection of our consciousness about life.
» Our past is not our present.
» Our thought is creative.
» Spirit is forever evolving and expanding through us.
» Spirit knows no obstruction.
» Spirit never contradicts its own nature.
» Spirit supports its own expression.
» Spirit withholds nothing from us.
» That which is visible is a manifestation of the invisible.
» That which we desire in our hearts is God's desire for us.
» That with which we identify becomes our experience.
» The Divine pattern seeks expression through each individual life.
» The Law knows neither big nor little.
» The Law of God, which is perfect, operates through us.
» The Law reflects our mental attitudes exactly as they are.
» The relationship we have with money is a reflection of the relationship we have with God.
» The truth of Being is God and humans are One.
» The universe is an orderly system.

» There are no mistakes in God's world, and God's world is all there is.
» There is a divine pattern of perfection at the center of all being, which has never been touched by disease or misfortune.
» There is no competition in Divine Expression.

In his book *Healing the Incurable,* Frederick Bailes wrote that when the knowledge of the power outweighs the fear of the condition, the person can be healed. So long as the fear of the condition outweighs the assurance of the Power, he cannot be healed (27). The term is not important. The key to the flow of this spiritual force is that the Source be contacted.

> *All healing is the result of individual consciousness, yours or mine. It is not dependent on God; it is not dependent on God-consciousness or Christ-consciousness in the abstract, but upon individual consciousness lifted to the heights of Christ-consciousness, which is the God-power that makes it possible to do the works of God.*
>
> Joel S. Goldsmith
> *The Art of Spiritual Healing* (82)

Chapter 14
ALIGNING THE FOCUS

The technique of Spiritual Mind Treatment is lifting the consciousness of the Practitioner into alignment with spiritual truth, and recognizing the client as Spirit always in perfect harmony with the image and likeness of God. This is the place where there is no one to be healed, just something to be realized, which is the client's true spiritual identity. For more effective treatment in setting Subjective Law in motion, some of the keys include

» Recognition of the sacredness of mental treatment
» Understanding that the Practitioner works through
   the Law of Mind
» A belief in perfect God, perfect man, and perfect being
» Knowing the truth that the spiritual client is perfect
» Elimination of any obstruction
» Knowing the client is now controlled by peace, love,
   and harmony
» Believing it is the nature of the Creative Power to take form
» Deep inner conviction that we are all Spirit

» No fear or doubt
» Knowing that we know
» Conviction that goodness is greater than any apparent opposite
» Pure realization of God in all
» And, in *The Science of Mind*, "The more completely the practitioner is convinced of the power of his own word, the more power his word will have. THERE MUST BE A RECOGNITION THAT THE POWER OF THE WORD, OPERATING AS THE TRUTH AND REALITY OF BEING, CAN DO ALL THINGS. Therefore, the person whose consciousness is the clearest, who has the most complete faith, will be the best healer" (170).

Complete faith is when the Practitioner can no longer deny the Truth. Jesus referred to doing a prayer of faith that would cause a creative law to reflect back to the ones praying, the situation and conditions corresponding to their beliefs—it is done unto you as you believe (Matthew 9:28).

> *Behind every condition is a belief, and if you can*
> *change the belief, you can change the condition.*
>
> Dr. Craig Carter
> *How to Use the Power of Mind* (4)

As Practitioners we work in our own mind until we are mentally satisfied and our whole mind understands that the client is healed. When this point occurs, Cause has been uncovered and truth revealed. At this moment it is time for a Spiritual Mind Treatment. The focus of the treatment is only ABOUT the client. The goal is to reinforce the belief the Practitioner has about the client, while the results begin and end in the consciousness of the Practitioner. This is how Law is set into motion. **All treatment must end in a realization, or it is just a bunch of words.**

Each treatment is unique to the client and is not used for anyone else. The Practitioner, like everything in nature, grows every day and is never in the same place in consciousness twice. Each treatment must meet the needs of individual clients. The Practitioner is the *vehicle* for the power of God, not *the* power of God. We are not the doer—God is the doer. Through treatment, we Practitioners open our consciousness about the client and the truth and power of our Christ or Universal consciousness, and end with a clear knowing about the client along with a personal sense of inner peace. We should have a new realization about God when the treatment is finished.

The goal of treatment for the Practitioner is to stand back in consciousness far enough to see both sides of the person's being. The Practitioner is clear that change and truth are available without sickness and disease. Treatment works independently of the Practitioner. Even if the client's issue is the same as the Practitioner's, each one has a different cause. Treatment does not will things to happen, but opens up an avenue within where it can happen:

> *Treatment must always have a specific end in view.*
> *Treatment begins and ends in the thought of the one*
> *giving the treatment. When it is finished in one place*
> *(the mind), it is finished everywhere.*

Dr. Raymond Charles Barker
Spiritual Healing for Today (77, 80)

In spiritual mind treatment, clients cease looking for answers in the past and release their fear of the future. Treatment brings new cause into their world and with it, a realization that they are their world. The first treatment should do all the work necessary to heal Cause, provided there is a complete realization by the Practitioner—a sensing, feeling, internalization. Treatment reunites the soul of the Practitioner with its Source. That is why there is a feeling of conviction and total trust. A treatment from the intellect of the Practitioner may be perfect in form, but will not be effective without these things. As Paul said, "Now faith is the substance of things hoped for, the evidence of things not seen" (Hebrews 11:1).

Treatment

In saying a treatment, the Practitioner invokes grace and spirit and works to change cause right at that moment. This changes the effect at some point in time and lets ego open the door, allowing grace to flow in. Verbal treatment helps reach the greater reality; ego mind opens up, letting meaningfulness come through.

Treatment has nothing to do with trying to concentrate the power of God; it already is. In treatment we permit, not petition; are positive, not negative; reach out to freedom and bliss, where there is no tension or struggle; allow a relaxed acceptance. Actually the words are not as important as the sincerity of the one giving it. The deficiencies in how well a treatment works are not in the words of the prayer, but in the conviction of the pray-er.

The treatment should have everything in it to cover the case. It is the business of the Practitioner to untie every mental knot, yet this does not mean giving direction to the client. We do not channel energy. Our energy is the same as the client's, and both are equally spiritual. There are simply different levels of awareness.

When using denial in treatment, we can say something like, "All limitations fall away." Denial can be used to cancel a limitation the clients have accepted and help them get their power back. If we use denial to take something away, we must be sure we replace it with truth. If our clients have excessive negativity or depression, we ask them to share two to three things they are thankful for, and in treatment appreciate the blessings in their life.

A demonstration is a manifestation. We cannot demonstrate beyond our ability to mentally embody an idea. It does not depend on location, environment, or condition—only on acceptance and belief. In cases of trauma and severe suffering, we know that suffering is not necessary. The soul of the client will know it is time to go on to other experiences and growth, that it is time to get better. We know that the soul knows what to do to get better and continue on its path of growth in this reality. It is the client's choice, and love is present to support his choice.

Disease will be healed, provided that we find cause and heal it, and that the person we are working with wants to surrender cause. Disease without thought could not manifest. The Practitioner turns from the condition and contemplates it as it ought to be, never as it appears to be. Clients are spiritually perfect and disease cannot attach itself to spirit. Our spiritual being is constantly remaking our physical being.

Here are some questions to ask if the goal of treatment is in question:

» Does this add to the client's ability to take action?
» Does it express a more abundant life?
» Does it take away from no one?
» Does it create no delusion?
» Does it express a greater degree of aliveness?

> *The Great Life Principle is always surging to express Itself and needs no coercion. It does, however, need direction, just as we would direct electricity or any other natural force.*
>
> Ernest Holmes
> *Lessons in Spiritual Mind Healing* (53)

Chapter 15
LIVING LIFE FULLY

According to Gandhi's grandson, when Gandhi developed his philosophy of nonviolence he was living in South Africa. He wanted an appropriate word to describe it, but he was having trouble finding one. At that point he decided a Sanskrit word might be appropriate since he was planning to move back to India and lead the Indian struggle for freedom. He decided the word "Satyagraha" described his philosophy the best. It is a combination of two Sanskrit words "Satya" meaning Truth and "Agraha" meaning insistence. Thus Satyagraha means the Truth Force. In this context, nonviolence is described as an honest pursuit of truth (Prabhu and Rao 682).

In living life fully, we find at times that life requires us to take constructive action, which means getting involved in finding constructive solutions to problems. We all have our own problems that need constructive solutions, but often we are so preoccupied with ourselves that we don't have time for anyone or anything else. When we are busy with life, it is very easy to put the responsibility for the larger problems on someone else's shoulders. Today that scapegoat is usually the government, but government's shoulders have severe limitations. Overall, our society wants government to do more than ever to make our lives comfortable, but I don't know how many government job descriptions include finding constructive solutions to violence. So by expecting someone else to solve the problems, a lot of really great ideas stay buried in the subconscious minds of those who hold back.

In *Treat Yourself to Life* Raymond Charles Barker writes about the Law of Averages: "If you fail to direct your subconscious mind, it produces your experience through the Law of Averages, and you are a nice, ineffective, sweet person" (84). Those who take potluck, who don't do anything evil because they were warned they would go to hell if they did, also don't do any good, because that takes effort, and they also become nice, sweet, and ineffective. That's what I love about Religious Science! We don't tell people *what* to think, we teach them *how* to think. How many places in our life are we nice, sweet, and ineffective?

Gandhi's website (http://www.mkgandhi.org) includes his favorite stories that deal with this issue of holding back. Here is one. There was an ancient king who was obsessed with the need to find the meaning of peace; what is peace; and how can we get it? And when we find it, what should we do with it? The wisest men in his kingdom were invited to answer the king's questions for a handsome reward. Many tried, but no one could explain how to find peace and what to do with it. At last someone suggested the king ought to consult a very old, wise sage who lived just outside the borders of his kingdom. The king went to the sage and posed the eternal question. Without a word the sage went into the kitchen and brought back a grain of wheat and said, "In this you will find the answer to your question," and he placed the grain of wheat in the king's outstretched palm. Unwilling to admit his ignorance the king clutched the grain of wheat and returned to his palace. He locked the grain in a tiny gold box and put it in his safe. Each morning the king would open the box and look at the grain to seek an answer, but he found nothing.

Weeks later another sage, passing through the area, stopped to meet the king who eagerly invited him to resolve his dilemma. The king explained how he had asked the eternal question and this sage gave him a grain of wheat instead. "I have been looking for an answer every morning but I find nothing." The sage said, "It is quite simple, your honor. Just as this grain represents nourishment for the body, peace represents nourishment for the soul. Now, if you keep this grain locked up in a gold box it will eventually perish without providing nourishment or multiplying. However, if it is allowed to interact with the elements—air, light, water, and soil—it will flourish, multiply, and soon you would have a whole field of wheat that will nourish not only you but many others. This is the meaning of peace. It must nourish your soul and the souls of others; it must multiply by interacting with the elements."

This means we need to play an active part in the world— part of the solutions. Perhaps we join in a community gathering in the park for peace. Everyone that attends is drawn there to be part of the solution. It is listening to that divine urge that God has given us . . . the urge for peace, the urge for love, the urge to help others.

In *The Science of Mind* text, Ernest Holmes describes the Divine Urge as that inner urge to push, drive, persuade (469).

It is a strong emotion. We live in a world of infinite possibilities where we have the co-creative power, the freedom, to choose a life where we just take "potluck" or we move our feet and take constructive action to find positive solutions to problems. I think sometimes we Religious Scientists get very complacent about community, state, national, or world problems. Ernest Holmes wrote,

> *We do not exist for the purpose of making an impression upon our environment. We do exist to express ourselves in and through our environment. We do not exist to leave a lasting impression upon our environment. It is not necessary that we leave any impression. It is not necessary, if we should pass on tonight, that anyone should remember that we have ever lived. All that means anything is that while we live, WE LIVE, and wherever we go from here that we keep on living. It is quite a burden lifted when we realize that we do not have to move the world—it is going to move anyway.*

(*Science of Mind* 270)

This realization does not lessen our duty or our social obligation. It clarifies it. You see, we don't have to bear the burden of the world—our challenge is to contribute to it as only we can. The truth is we can do this joyously and free from morbidity or sorrow.

Religious Science teaches that God can do no more for us than He can do through us. We are dynamic expressions of God in this life's journey. We are dynamic expressions of God in our quest to know the truth, and through our co-creative ability we naturally connect with Spirit. We are here to release something in ourselves that is bigger than we previously imagined. In our quest for truth and contributing positively to our adventure of life, it takes strength and courage.

Dr. Raymond Charles Barker wrote in *Treat Yourself to Life,* "Success is not based on grandiose achievements or the applause of the public. The successful individual is creative in their experience, and is at peace with themselves. A failure is anyone who, either through their own ignorance or acceptance of a situation that seems out of their control, has resigned themselves to some form of expression which is frustrating rather than creative" (70).

I was at a meeting where a doctor gave a PowerPoint presentation on his contribution to world peace by serving in Doctors Without Borders. Founded in 1971, this organization is an unofficial arm of the French government and is part of its foreign policy outreach program. It has over 4,000 volunteers working in forty-five countries; its motto is "One Earth–One Family." These doctors believe nothing should prevent those needing health care from receiving it. In the world today, over 50 percent of their work is done is treating combat casualties.

Some of the locations where this particular doctor had served included Chechnya, East Timor, Ramallah, Gaza City, Afghanistan, Somalia, Iraq, and Kosovo. On one of his trips, he rotated every two to three weeks through several refugee camps and medical centers. He was in Chechnya when it was in Russian control, and the Russian Army transported his group wherever they needed to go. In the camp where he served on the Chechen border, there were anywhere from 20,000 to 30,000 refugees.

About 1,000 arrived every day—and about 1,000 died every day. The predominant injury was phosphorus burns from Russian mortars. On this trip, there was often so little medical aid available that all they could do was stabilize the ones who had a good chance of surviving and ship them off to a medical center, "while the rest," he said, "were left outside in the rain to die."

Someone asked the doctor if there was any religious presence at all in the refugee camps. He said no. Did the refugees complain or protest about their care? He said no, that the people were very simple, and all they wanted was to work their land and be left alone. Someone asked if the doctor had seen Mel Gibson's movie, *The Passion*. Yes, he had. Did it affect him at all? No, not really, but he said it was like working a shift in an ER trauma unit, and hard to watch because he couldn't get up and help. That Divine urge, the divine urge in all of us, is to help one another.

The doctor showed us a picture of a fourteen-year-old Russian soldier in his uniform. My eyes were riveted on this photo, a handsome young man wearing a bandolier of bullets and holding a rifle. He wasn't smiling, but had a peaceful look on his face. The doctor spent many hours with this young fellow while they traveled from one camp to another. The boy could speak good English, which was his third language. He asked the doctor about the status of the International Monetary Fund, decisions at the United Nations, about the Palestinians and Israelis, and other world issues. The doctor was very impressed with the interest this intelligent teenager had in world events. He found out four days later that the young man had been killed by a sniper's bullet.

Someone lamented that they wished the doctor had not told us the young man had been killed so we could have been left with the image of his picture. But it's reality; this is what the rest of the world is dealing with. It is hard for some people to accept the pain and suffering going on in the world today, but that unwillingness to see, supports an inability to act. If you can't see suffering, you won't find the inner strength to help. If peace is going to be, it is up to us, every one of us. It is up to all of us collectively to take constructive action, in whatever way that works for us. Peace begins in our conscious mind and, through belief and acceptance, it moves into our subconscious mind where the co-creative action of Spirit, of God, brings it into being.

Constructive action toward peace means moving away from greed, self-centeredness, and possessiveness to greater love, compassion, understanding, and respect. It is up to each of us to decide if we are going to let the Law of Averages run our life. Will we be sweet, nice, and ineffective, or will we make good use of the gifts Spirit has given us and allow everything we have, inside and out, to interact positively with the elements of our world and help create a society of peace and harmony?

We all can't be doctors, but we can all respond to events by sharing what we believe. It is not in our religion to proselytize, but it is in our religion to speak the truth. As Practitioners in training, we go forth and let Spirit guide us. Remember, we live in a universe of infinite possibilities.

Gandhi led the Indian struggle for freedom and won. Problems are the beginning of solutions. The problems of the world are here because the human race is trying to find out how to live in peace. It won't happen if we just sit back and watch. Treat and move your feet. Every one of us can play a bigger part in achieving world peace than we currently are. We have many great examples. Follow Gandhi, follow Raymond Charles Barker or Ernest Holmes. Let the co-creative nature of God's gift to the world, which is you, take constructive action in some way today.

Chapter 16

EXERCISES FOR CLARITY

There are times when using an exercise with a client may get to Cause in a much more meaningful way. Here are a few ideas.

THERE IS ALWAYS SOMETHING TO BE THANKFUL FOR

For clients with depression or severe negativity, we can ask them to share what they are thankful for. The power is in doing this for three minutes without stopping. Then we focus the treatment on appreciation for these blessings. A shift in attitude can occur through gratitude.

THE PATH TO THE PRESENT

Ask the clients to choose a part of life and describe what is happening in that area. Ask what five stepping stones brought them to this position. Ask them to meditate to a point of rest on these steps and then write a dialogue between themselves and that area of life. Look for insights and areas of mistaken beliefs.

ZEN CLOCK

Draw two circles on a paper. These are two faces of a clock. In the first one, segment the clock by the amount of time they spend doing necessary things in their life, such as working, sleeping, playing, exercising, or reading. Use the second clock face to segment the time they would rather spend on each activity. Focus on changing Cause so that they can create the effect of the second clock face in their life.

TRUTH MADE EASY

Getting clients back on the path of truth may be easier if they can identify areas in which they can contribute love to the world. Using a paper and pen, let them list the many ways they could do this, and then brainstorm ideas on how they could make some of those things happen.

BE HAPPY

One of the easiest ways clients can increase the level of happiness in their life is to

1. Decide to be happy
2. Stop complaining
3. Find things to praise
4. Pay attention when they start hearing negative thoughts in their mind or hearing negative words coming from their mouth; change it at once to positive and creative ideas
5. Begin to do something new and different

EXPAND INTUITION

Intuition can be strengthened by experience. Troward wrote that if, in spite of all appearances pointing us in a direction of conduct, there is still a persistent feeling that we should not do something, more often than not, we shall be successful following our intuition (*Edinburgh Lectures* 63). Why? We may not have conscious knowledge at the time, but it is the Law of Attraction and our subjective knowledge that is at work. Ask clients to talk about times when they did not listen to their intuition and ended up with a negative experience. Discuss the benefit of meditation and how it allows that inner voice to surface. Ask how they might make more of an effort to hear that voice.

WHERE IS THE STRESS?

If clients are feeling unsatisfied and unfulfilled, but are not sure where the problem lies, ask them to indicate their level of satisfaction in the following areas, followed by the level of importance (high, medium and low) they attach to each one: need, sexuality, friendship, being loved, loving others, self-esteem, creative achievement, spirituality, respect of peers, excitement and challenge, quiet and peaceful, security in work, and an intimate long-term relationship. The areas identified as high importance with low satisfaction are the ones to focus on in the search for Cause.

WHO AM I

Each person plays a number of roles in life such as friend, mother, father, aunt, neighbor, leader, etc. How we describe our relationship to each of these roles can be an indicator where change is needed. Too often we wait for people or things in life to change, but if we change, then those other things or people will also change. Ask the clients to list all the roles they play and attach an adjective to each of the roles that best describes their relationship with it. Those roles with negative connotations are the areas that need change. Through the use of Principle and Law, show clients how they can become the thing they wish to demonstrate.

THE BODY AS AN INDICATOR OF MENTAL EQUIVALENT

The body is a spiritual idea and every part of it is significant. There will be times when a Practitioner can see a client's body reflecting back to her an area in need of work. Can the client translate the physical malfunction to a mental or emotional equivalent? Some of the mental equivalents include

Arm	=	embracing or releasing a situation
Body total	=	the sum total of conscious and unconscious ideas
Ear	=	sensing truth and understanding
Elbow	=	changing directions
Eye	=	perceiving truth
Face	=	facing truth
Finger	=	grasping details
Head	=	knowing truth
Heart	=	power, love, joy
Knee	=	flexibility
Legs	=	moving forward
Lungs	=	taking in the knowledge of God
Mouth	=	praising and responding
Neck	=	flexibility
Stomach	=	digesting and assimilating or eliminating ideas
Thumb	=	grasping ideas for comparison

WHAT IS AN ATTITUDE?

An "attitude" often develops when a bad habit has continued so long that it turns positive personal qualities into negative ones. Again we can find pairs of opposites. Can your client figure out the positive expression, the truth that is being blocked by any of these negative attitudes: blame, envy, fear, prejudice, selfishness, self-pity, jealousy, criticism, judgment, anger, inferiority, confusion, self-doubt, resentment, worry, guilt, procrastination, competition.

RELEASE AND LET GO

Sometimes we bombard ourselves with negative messages that block our ability to move forward. These are often in the form of "I believe I should . . ." or "I believe I must . . ." statements. Ask clients to list all of their "should" and "musts." Why do they feel that way? What has kept them from doing each one? If they accomplish a *should* or a *must,* how will it make them feel? Does it still feel important? If not, release it and let it go.

PATHWAYS TO BLISS

The Law of Giving and Receiving is always at work in our lives. If clients are focused on how they can receive, it may be useful to ask how they can give. Here are a few ideas on opportunities to give:

» How can I add more value to my immediate environment?
» What small decision can I make today to increase joy and happiness for someone?
» How can I be vulnerable in this situation?
» What small gift can I give others right now to melt a barrier or break the tension?
» How can I communicate more clearly to get the other person to understand me?

» In what way can I give others more of what I need?
» What can I say to let the other person feel valued and listened to?
» In what way can I show someone I value him as a person?
» What can I say to encourage others to be honest and ask for what they want?
» How can I show others I value their friendship?
» In what way can I express my desire to encourage others to be who they really are?
» How can I encourage my friends to open up and allow their creative energy to flow?
» How can I show others that just being alive can be a love affair with the Universe?

· →≫≫≫ ·

Chapter 17
COMPASSION WITH ACTION

· ≪≪≪← ·

Not a day goes by that we aren't called upon to help one another, even in the smallest way. Yet when someone's need is great, often we might think, "What is it that really helps?" Compassion is a gift that can be given at any point in time, and it is always helpful in one way or another.

What is compassion? Webster says it's a sympathetic consciousness about others' suffering with a desire to alleviate it; kindness; pity. Ram Dass, a great spiritual teacher, says that compassion is the tender opening of our hearts to pain and suffering. He says when we see suffering, we see the parts of life we often push away, things that cause us sadness, anger or outrage. Yet, when we open our hearts to pain and suffering and become familiar with them, we are more likely to hear ways to respond with love and support to relieve the suffering (*How Can I Help?* 14).

The Religious Science definition of demonstrating compassion is bringing our deepest truth into our actions, no matter how much the world seems to resist it; to bring loving kindness into each situation in which we find ourselves.

Because caring is an automatic reflex, when we are in the presence of pain and suffering, we often feel the call to jump in and fix things. Usually, however it is important to be quiet and listen to find what we can really do to help. When we hear the cry of pain, whether it is from a person, a family or a whole community, in order to continue to live honestly with ourselves and others, we naturally want to respond. We are generally rewarded for giving through acknowledgment, recognition, respect, but often giving is tied with expecting to receive something. Spiritually speaking, as Religious Scientists, we know giving to others simply for personal recognition is not compassion.

There is a list of things to avoid saying to someone whose spouse recently died. Avoid saying things like It was God's will . . . I know just how you feel . . . God picks the most beautiful flowers first . . . We are never given more than we can handle . . . God needs him or her more than you do . . . They lived a good full life and it was their time to go. Well, then, what do we say? How can we be compassionate and say something helpful? It does get confusing to understand where true compassion begins.

When do we know we are being compassionate?

Years ago, I completed a Chaplain Training Course at Redding Medical Center with its chaplain, Father Art Lillicropp. Fr. Art was a very colorful character: forty-five years old, an Episcopalian priest from Boston who was once blind but thanks to two eye transplants could now see perfectly. He was compassion in action personified. Our class had fifteen people and included Baptists, Seventh Day Adventists, Church of Christ members, Episcopalians, and five Religious Scientists.

I thought being a chaplain meant visiting the sick and praying with them, giving them love and encouragement, and they would smile and thank us for coming. But early on, Fr. Art rattled our assumptions. He gave us a case history from his experience in Boston and asked the class what we as chaplain associates would do. What would you do?

> A twenty-six-year-old man with Downs Syndrome was brought in from a group home. He was phobic, in chronic pain, and unable to express himself. He had been attending a Baptist church. The diagnosis was inoperable leukemia. The choices were aggressive chemo, hospice, or radiation.

Question—What does the patient want? What do we do? The Baptists immediately raised their hands and said "pray." No, Fr. Art said. The first thing to do is smile, connect with his eyes, be attentive in order to help reduce his level of anxiety and fear. Meet the immediate needs of the patient and his family, if possible. Offer support and comfort. Then, in talking with the people who brought him in, find the person who can communicate best with him and share this information with the staff. Only when we have developed a level of trust with the patient, do we enter the area of their personal beliefs. After that, praying is done only with the patient's consent.

> In another case, an unconscious eighty-five-year-old woman was brought in by helicopter. No family came along. It looked like a heart attack. In her purse were no advance directives, and no insurance card, just a basic ID. The ER stabilized her and she was taken to the Intensive Care Unit where she coded—her heart

stopped beating. The doctors had just taken the woman into surgery when her family, who were Jehovah's Witnesses, arrived. The staff asked the chaplain to meet with the family.

Question: What do you do? Try to understand how they are feeling, if they understand the diagnosis. Attend to their needs and just be present.

In a hospital, the staff is "fix" oriented. The chaplain's work is a ministry of listening, attending, and presence. We listen for the patients' base fears and stay awake to the suffering. It is sometimes the way in which God's purposes are achieved. It is their journey; they lead us where they need to go. Just by being present we increase their awareness of God's presence in their lives. When we visit patients, it is their needs that come first, not our desire to do something or even pray. Like Fr. Art said, it is their journey, they lead us where they need to go. We can't always make them happy, no matter how much we want to, but we can create an environment in which wholesome choices are more likely to be made. We can help patients gain insight and skill so they feel they have more control over their lives, less anxiety, and more peace. This wasn't quite the picture I had in my mind about chaplain work.

I'm finally realizing what true compassion is, and it is not easy to do. Of course, in Religious Science language, we say it is getting easier all the time. And for a Religious Scientist to be compassionate during strong emotional events might be easier for us than others, because we know God is all there is; there is a reason for everything; there is a seed of growth in the pain. Yet, when we want to say the right thing to help relieve pain, it is often to help relieve our own pain and our discomfort with the situation.

We feel powerless and vulnerable, but it is through feeling powerless and vulnerable that we find our true strength—the strength that only God can provide.

So compassion comes down to two things: 1) Intent. When we are called upon to be compassion in action, we think about the intent of our words and actions. Compassion is not trying to solve the problems of the person who is suffering. It is compassionate to accompany him on his journey and do what you can to help make him comfortable. As Ernest Holmes wrote, "Health is a mental as well as a physical state. Each person will deliver themselves from sickness and trouble in exact proportion to the discovery of the self and their true relationship to the whole" (*Science of Mind* 190). What greater gift can we as Religious Scientists give to those in suffering than our presence and knowing the perfection in the patient. 2) Equanimity. Equanimity is a valuable quality. It is that inner peace we find during meditation. It is that inner peace we feel when we've learned to be in a hectic situation and let go of our expectations and see all before us as God in action. It is all right and just as it should be. When we bring equanimity to any situation, our heart stays open in the presence of the suffering of others. We learn not to be afraid of heartbreak. We are part of the family of human beings with all of the joys and sadness.

> *My heart's desire is to create an open space for God*
> *to express through me; to empty myself of myself so*
> *that God can fill me up.*
>
> From a chaplain's prayer
> written by Chaplain Gretchen TenBrook
> in *Broken Bodies, Healing Hearts* (x)

Chapter 18
CASE STUDIES

CASE STUDY #1

A church member was experiencing intense fear about her health. She had been suffering frequent arthritis pain, continuous infection of the mouth, and chest pains brought on by emphysema. She was taking medication for stomach problems and sleeping only two hours a night. As her condition worsened, she was feeling a great deal of sadness and anger.

The Practitioner found Cause to be a lack of self-love and unworthiness. The treatment focus was harmony and love, trusting the Law to achieve perfect health in its own way.

After treatment work with a Practitioner, her life really changed. She said, "I realized that I am not inherently evil, and I have nothing to fear. I am truly an individual, unique expression of God, Love, and Good. The result of this sudden, dramatic revelation is that for the first time, I expect as much from myself as I do from everyone else. I came face to face with my doubts and fears, which were mostly about my health, and we met them head on with Truth and treatment."

She went on to say, "Arthritis seems to run in my family and it was crippling all of us. My pain was getting worse than ever. On the day of the treatment work, I was in severe pain. I have had no arthritis pain since then. In addition, my chest is now remarkably free of pain. My sleeping pattern has gone from two hours a night to five or six hours."

Four months later, she was still pain free and had no further need for the medications she had taken for years. A previously diagnosed ulcer also disappeared. She also had a fungus infection on her foot, which was never discussed at the treatment session, and it disappeared. Interestingly enough, exactly the same condition had been present on the Practitioner's foot, and that, too, was healed.

CASE STUDY #2

A client sought assistance from a Practitioner regarding work and prosperity. He had been in and out of work, which was creating chaos in his family. During the interview, the Practitioner found Cause to be a disregard for life as God in action. The treatment focus was Love as Law.

After treatment, he reported, "Much to my surprise, I found out that my real need was for inner peace. After the treatment, I could feel a change in my consciousness, which amazed me. Later that day, a friend called to tell me about a job, but when I went in the next morning, his boss said that he couldn't hire me. Normally, anxiety and fear of lack of money would have taken over, but to my surprise, I was calm, content, and peaceful.

"That evening, another friend called me about work. When I showed up the next morning, his boss also turned me down. Again, I was calm and peaceful—not worried. That night, one of my friends called again and said that I should come in the next day. This time, the boss hired me.

"Throughout these three days of uncertainty, I was able to remain unaffected by these conditions. My mind automatically chose peace and contentment, even though I was completely aware of everything that was happening."

CASE STUDY #3

A church member sought the help of a Practitioner because she was suffering a lot of pain over an old relationship. She was having extreme difficulty putting that person out of her mind. The Practitioner found Cause to be the fear of not being enough. Treatment focus was being pure love and pure light.

After the treatment, she reported, "I have suddenly realized that I want to have a relationship with myself so that I can better understand my own thinking and emotions and avoid all the fear, hurt, and pain that develop when I move too fast in a relationship. The really great part about this experience is that I am seeing a change in my thinking. I am aware of my feelings, yet I am making conscious and rational decisions about what I want to do. The pain over my prior relationship has gone away."

Dr. Ernest Holmes wrote that the healing process—insofar as it may be termed a process—is in becoming conscious of the Eternal Truth: our lives are none other than the Life of God (*Science of Mind* 161).

Chapter 19

LIFE AS I WANT IT

Science of Mind Class 207 is based on Thomas Troward's book *The Edinburgh Lectures on Mental Science,* which was originally published in 1904. Troward can be difficult to understand since he writes in the language of an Englishman at the turn of the century. In class, the teacher doesn't do as much lecturing as facilitating a discussion and understanding of Troward's concepts. So if his writings are so hard to understand, why is this class required for students of Science of Mind? One reason is that Ernest Holmes, the founder of Religious Science and the author of our text, *The Science of Mind,* said that about 25 percent of his writings and ideas came from Troward.

Troward lived from 1847 to 1916. Born in Punjab, India, of British parents, he spent his formative years in school in England. He graduated from college with gold medal honors in literature. Then he passed the Indian Civil Service Examination and became a judge in Punjab for twenty-five years. When he retired, he moved his family back to England and immersed himself in studying and writing about mental science and painting. He was one of the original philosophers that contributed to what became known around the turn of the century as New Thought.

Ernest Holmes was born in 1887 in New England, and thanks to his mother, he developed a keen interest in spiritual studies. At age eighteen he moved to Boston and began a career as a platform speaker. About this time he discovered Ralph Waldo Emerson, whose writings were a major source of inspiration. He was introduced to Christian Science and attended lectures given by Mary Baker Eddy where he learned about mental healing. Although he was never known to be a member of Christian Science, he practiced the prayer treatment technique and eventually reformulated it and called it Spiritual Mind Treatment.

In 1912, at age twenty-five, he moved to California to live with his brother Fenwick, a Congregational minister living in Venice. Holmes took a job with the city. About that time he came across Thomas Troward's writings, which he said eclipsed anything he had ever read. Holmes said, "Troward's writings are the most profound spiritual abstractions of modern times" (Vahle 47). Reading Troward gave him further insight into the techniques of mental healing and the theory behind it.

Holmes studied the writings of great spiritual teachers, the world's most sacred texts, and writings of the philosophers from our country including Phineas Parkhurst Quimby, Ralph Waldo Emerson, Ralph Waldo Trine, Horatio Dresser, Emma Curtis Hopkins, whom Holmes called an illumined soul, and others including Thomas Troward. Holmes was so well versed in spiritual texts and the New Thought philosophy, it wasn't long before he was invited to give small lessons in mental healing, which blossomed into speaking engagements to thousands of people each Sunday, and the rest is history. It is a great story that you can read about in Neal Vahle's book *Open at the Top*.

When asked about the Science of Mind philosophy, Dr. Holmes said his contribution was only to simplify it, refine it, divest it of superstition, and give it an actual sequence of steps. He reduced all the theory into a definite concept that could be practiced. He believed life can be like you want it by learning the Laws of the Universe, the implications of the Law of Cause and Effect, the power of Love and Law, and the technique of Spiritual Mind Treatment.

In a class years ago, we were asked to write an essay entitled, My Ideal and Perfect Day. At first I thought it would be easy, but as I began to write, I found myself wadding up my papers and thinking, if it's going to be perfect, surely it can be better than that! I thought—here it is—my opportunity to create the most absolutely perfect day ever—when I could do absolutely anything I wanted to do, wherever I wanted to do it, with anyone I wanted to do it with. It took a dozen or so renditions over the course of a week before I could read my essay and comfortably say yes, this is it. I saved the essay all these years, and I think one reason is that the teacher wrote across the top, "Wow! Can I have your day?"

Since that time, there have been many days when I can honestly say it happened; I had my ideal and perfect day. I didn't realize it as it was happening, but the next day when I reflected on it, there it was: my ideal and perfect day. It's always an awesome feeling. On the spiritual journey, you can create life like you want it and enjoy more perfect days.

Thanks to Troward and Holmes, we believe there is an originating power and presence in the Universe that we call God or Spirit. We know we exist, and we exist as individuals with volition, the power of choice, the power to make decisions. We observe nature and see that humans and everything around us are a product of eons and eons of evolution. We believe this is the way God knows Itself, by becoming everything and expanding and evolving into infinity.

Today science affirms Troward's writings that the Universe is expanding, growing, evolving. Remember the last time you were in a museum and looked at the furniture from a century or so ago? People were a lot smaller. Recently there was a photo of a baby born that weighed over sixteen pounds! And those basketball players that are seven feet tall! We can see the product of evolution in our own lifetime. We're an integral part of this evolving and growing universe. Would you like be back at the time when you were sixteen years old? Most of us would say no, not without the knowledge we have now. We're learning to live our lives consciously instead of being unconscious, oblivious to God's nature. I sure wouldn't want to let go of that just to have a cute figure.

We have a conscious mind; it is the one that got us up this morning, made breakfast, and got us dressed. And we have a subconscious mind, the one that contains our intuition. It is that place where we have an intimate connection with God. It might help to think of these as the outer mind and the inner mind.

Troward wrote that when our outer thoughts are strong enough, they create a nucleus, a seed in our subconscious or inner mind, and if the seed is allowed to grow undisturbed, through the Laws of the Universe it will eventually attract all the conditions necessary to manifest or show up in visible form

(*Edinburgh Lectures* 31). The seeds of our thought are like little magnets, and each seed we plant is a prototype. If we plant the seed of love, it attracts to itself all the things necessary to show up as love in our life just like a magnet. This is what is meant by Cause and Effect. Cause is the belief in our inner mind that shows up as the effect, the thing or experience we have. To have life like we want it, for instance our ideal and perfect day, we must plant that seed in our inner mind and let it grow. For example, to have a big red ripe tomato for our ham sandwich, a tomato seed had to be planted. That seed has in it all that it needed to create a tomato. The seed was watered and had lots of sun, God's love, and it grew naturally. We don't instantly get big red ripe tomatoes; we get a sprout, then leaves, then a blossom, then a green tomato, and if everything continues in a healthy pattern, we get to enjoy the juicy taste of a big red ripe, perfect tomato. If along the way we don't water the seed, or we let weeds grow up and choke it, or if it doesn't get enough light, you know what happens—we have to go buy somebody else's tomato and hope it gives us the same satisfying results.

According to Troward, mental science depends on using the Law of Growth, and growth occurs from the vitality inherent in the entity itself (*Edinburgh Lectures* 35). Tomatoes grow from the vitality inherent in the tomato seed. It will always grow into a tomato, not a carrot or a potato. We cannot make a tomato seed become a carrot by using our willpower. A tomato seed is a prototype, just as a belief or thought we place in our inner mind is a prototype. Troward wrote that the greater vitality we put into the spiritual prototype, the quicker it will germinate, but if we are in a hurry and anxious, we form an opposite spiritual prototype that destroys the first one. It is like planting a tomato seed and then pulling it out of the ground the next day to see how it's doing. It's like setting a cause in motion, placing an idea seed in our inner mind, and then we reverse it. The same law that produces positive results from positive thoughts also produces negative effects from negative thoughts. It's the Law. Troward calls this the Variable Factor (37). We are the Variable Factor. Our outer mind is the Variable Factor. The Invariable Factor is the Law of Growth. Tomato seed grows into a tomato plant. Our inner mind creates our experiences by the Law of Growth. Every day our life is different because our ideas, our beliefs are different. So how do we have more experiences that feel like an ideal and perfect day?

According to Troward, if we wish to create ideal and perfect days, we must be willing to actively participate in the evolutionary process. It sounds like a big responsibility, so how do we do that? We consciously plant positive healthy seeds in mind and water those seeds. We are the guardian at the gate of our mind. Troward wrote that the increase in our creative power *must* be in exact proportion to our perception, our belief, of our relationship to Universal Mind, God. This originating spirit is light, love and beauty. The creative work of our thoughts brings us either closer to that experience or further away (46). Though we can never be separated from God, it sure can look that way sometimes.

In *My Personal Recollections of Thomas Troward*, Harry Gaze put together a lot of stories and anecdotes about Troward and his family, which included a wonderful wife and six children. Gaze relates that he was a wonderful father. In 1915 when his son Rupert went into the service and was being sent to the front in WWI, Troward wrote him a letter, and here is part of it:

> Put your whole trust in Him and fear not. It means a constant dwelling in thought upon the continual presence of God with us and around us. It is sort of constant conversation with God in our heart—nothing too good for Him to do for us and nothing of ours too small for Him to take notice. (45)

Troward suggested to his son,

> Your daily prayer should therefore be simply this: "Let me find Thee this day in myself." And then go forward in the full confidence that this prayer has been answered. This is not vain repetition but the highest operation of the Law of Cause and Effect. (45)

Years ago when I wrote about my ideal and perfect day, it was such an intense experience for me, I think it planted a powerful seed in my inner mind, that area where I connect with God. Apparently I've been watering it, because I've had more of these days. Is it my experience every day? No, I think of it somewhat like the seasons or the tides. My mind is full of really great spiritual things, and then it gets full of the everyday frustrations of life. But what Holmes helped me realize about my ideal and perfect day is that it was based on feelings of intense love; like he wrote, love is at the center of our being and the calm, continuous, pulsations of life are governed by Love (*Science of Mind* 238). So, are you curious? Here it is:

My Perfect Day

The sun peeks over the ridgetop and bathes the hillside and lake with morning light. The gray ambience in the bedroom is replaced with Dreamsicle orange. I awake and smile, watching the silhouette of branches from the oak tree paint an oriental picture on the curtains. I look at my lover and stroke the soft skin of his back. He turns and pulls me close. We cuddle for minutes before the energy growing between us reaches a crescendo and we make love. At rest, our limbs are entwined like spaghetti. Then we rise, shower, and let the pulsating water renew our spirit.

I squeeze oranges for juice and prepare a breakfast of muffins and fruit. In robes we sit on the patio by the lake in the glow of the sun, reading the paper and listening to the water lap against the side of our boat tied at the dock. Seagulls fly low; birds sing sweetly. Soft music flows from the stereo.

We dress casually and go exploring, either along the beach looking for new things that have washed up on shore, or venturing out in the boat to see what's happening elsewhere. The breeze blows through our hair. My lungs fill with fresh spring air. We return home with new treasures—shells, driftwood, and unique rocks.

Late morning is time for me to go to the study and express in words on the computer the energies that have built up that day. I write for a few hours on a story or script, churning out several pages of creative thought. He uses this time to do what feels good for him. Midafternoon we share a light snack on the patio or on the back deck of the boat and talk. We become totally focused on the pure enjoyment of our togetherness. Afterwards he sleeps, but my energy level has been renewed. I play the piano for an hour or so. When he wakes, he comes and listens to the music.

It is time to check on others who are important to us. We telephone distant friends and relatives to hear about their activities. We cherish the close, loving relationship we have with these people. Now we are ready to visit with local friends for the evening, to share their thoughts, feelings, goals, and aspirations. This may be a party, dinner at someone's home, theater, concert, or dancing. It keeps our minds in close touch with reality by hearing different opinions on things that may be critical or trivial and to share life's experience. We don't always agree with someone on a subject, but we appreciate their honesty and conviction. In this atmosphere, discussion on any subject becomes multidimensional. At the end of the evening, we leave feeling enriched.

Arriving home we wind down by reading, listening to the stereo or watching an old movie. I give my lover a massage from head to toe. His serene response gives me great pleasure. We snuggle up under warm covers awhile before turning over and falling off into a dreamless, peaceful night of rest. And so it is.

I encourage you to take some time and write down your ideal and perfect day. Think about it—the sounds, the smells, the beauty, the love. What's there and what isn't? Who's there and who isn't? Then, when you get it all figured out, plant that seed with the love and the knowledge of co-creation that you've gained in this teaching, and let the Law of Growth bring it forth perfectly.

Chapter 20

PROFESSIONALISM

Fundamental to the success of individual member centers and societies is the credibility and integrity of the conduct of their ministers, leaders, and Practitioners. Because they are representatives of their organization, those licensed by the organization must demonstrate a high degree of ethical conduct and professional integrity.

The policies of licensing organizations, such as Centers for Spiritual Living, include a Code of Ethics for Practitioners. These policies are established to govern the conduct of Practitioners in the area of ethical and professional conduct. Consequently, the policies are to be interpreted and applied by the licensing organizations and are not open to interpretation by individual Practitioners.

Practitioners do not support, encourage, promote, endorse, practice or teach anything that can be construed to mean that The Creative Power operates beyond the consciousness of the individual; or that more of The Creative Power resides in one individual than another; or that The Creative Power is directed by any means other than thought. This is directed specifically toward any kind of support for or use of gurus, mediums or channelers who claim to have special spiritual wisdom transmittable only through them, or special contact sources of wisdom unavailable to any individual through the use of his or her own consciousness. It also includes any kind of support for or use of any kind of inanimate objects such as crystals, pyramids, charms, or amulets as a means of bringing The Creative Power into activity in the consciousness of the individual. It does not, however, preclude the discussion of these matters for educational purposes, providing that such discussions are not construed to be either promotion or an endorsement.

Practitioners do not at the public level make derogatory or critical remarks about the integrity or ability of licensing organizations, their elected or appointed leaders, or of any of their fellow Practitioners. This means from any public platform, including their own center services or classes. This includes statements made on recordings or in writing intended for publication or sale. This is not to discourage complaints or dissent, but to encourage that such be addressed openly through legitimate channels.

Practitioners do not use vulgar language or offensive humor in making public presentations from their own or any other platform. What constitutes vulgar language or offensive humor is always open to interpretation; however, should the matter become an issue or complaint, the opinion of the licensing organization will be decisive.

Practitioner licenses are granted to qualified individuals whose sole spiritual commitment is to the teaching of the Science of Mind and the practice of Spiritual Mind Treatment under the

Policy and Bylaws of the licensing organizations and in service to their member churches.

A Practitioner operates under the authority and license granted by the organization for the purpose of practicing and disseminating the principles of Science of Mind and acts in a manner reflecting such principles. The speech and conduct of a Practitioner always reflect the dignity of this high profession. A Practitioner is advised to stay up-to-date on the policies and procedures of the licensing organization.

· →≫≫≯ ·

Chapter 21

STAYING ON THE PATH

· ≼≪≪← ·

We come to the Centers for Spiritual Living for answers, opportunities for spiritual growth, and to generate greater happiness and prosperity in our lives. We take classes, workshops, and retreats, all for the purpose of growing in spiritual awareness. The spiritual path is the most profound path we can walk, and it is amazing how long it takes some of us to step through the doors of a Center and discover this profound philosophy. Once we do, our life improves, but staying on the path can be a challenge.

When we make a personal commitment to walk the path of spiritual growth, the next challenge is to stay on it long enough to experience the benefits of an intimate connection with God, the universal creative power. It says in Matthew 7:7, "Ask, and it shall be given you; seek, and ye shall find; knock, and it shall be opened unto you."

We learn this is the truth, and one of the catalysts to make it work in our life is Spiritual Mind Treatment, our form of affirmative prayer. In our text *The Science of Mind,* Ernest Holmes wrote,

When we use our creative imagination in strong faith, it will create for us, out of the One Substance, whatever we have formed in thought. In this way we become Co-Creators with God. There will never be an end of the eternal verities like Truth, Love, Beauty. There will never be an end to God, nor to any of the attributes which are co-eternal and co-existent with God. If we are wise, we shall cultivate a faith in these realities. This is not a difficult task, but a thrilling experience! (157)

Yet, though most of us who have been on the path for a long time know this truth, we can still find ourselves wandering into the desert.

On occasional Sundays we can rationalize sleeping in. Sleeping in can be a good thing. The ego mind says, "Heck, I've come a long way, I'm even teaching classes. I don't need to hear so much about God and the law of the Universe anymore; the weeds in my front yard need my attention, and there's a good mystery book on the coffee table, so I'm taking the day off." Sounds rational, but over time when the ego gets puffed up, the sanctuary is exactly where we need to be on Sunday morning. Otherwise, by the middle of the week we're going faster and faster to keep up with our schedule, we're more judgmental, we have less patience with people, and another indicator, we think we need a shopping spree, the heck with the Visa bill. Hopefully it's not much longer before we're conscious that we've wandered off the path, not into something awful, but into activities that are draining and use our time for things that are more outward focused, more stuff focused. By the time our mind finally says, "Hey!" there can be a tangible feeling of separation, and the last time we felt truly connected with God-Spirit seems like a dream.

That's when it is time to pull ourselves back on the path. It can mean getting out *The Science of Mind* textbook and reading the profound wisdom of Ernest Holmes, reading treatments in the *Science of Mind* magazine, meditating, chanting, even when we're brushing our teeth. Then those words come back to us all day whenever we're not thinking about other things. It's the most effective way to do what the ancients taught—pray ceaselessly.

Raymond Holliwell's book *Working with the Law* is pleasantly surprising because of the many gems it contains, and many of these may be helpful with this issue of staying on the path. The chapter on the Law of Supply is one of his best. The first sentence reads "Man is never satisfied" (43). His book was written decades ago, so he meant "Mankind is never satisfied." At first it seems a shame that we are never satisfied, but Holliwell's second sentence is an eye opener: "God did not intend that we should be forever satisfied." Wait a minute, can that be true? Isn't it why we're on the spiritual path to get to that place where everything is just great all the time? Then his third sentence sets us straight: "The law of God's being is perpetual increase, progress and growth, so that when one good is realized, another desire for greater good will develop. The advancing life is the true life, the life that God intended us to live." It is true that the Universe continues to expand, the roses and trees continue to grow, return to the soil, and grow again. It is the creative power of the universe that continually creates new and better organisms. Holliwell's discerning point is that it is too easy to look to *things* as the source of our good instead of God, the creative force in the universe. This is the challenge: What comes first, seeing or believing? The Law is founded on our belief, which then determines our supply. Believing comes first (44).

Jesus said, "What things ye desire, when ye pray, believe that ye receive them and ye shall have them" (Mark 11:24). Ernest Holmes devised a form of affirmative prayer called Spiritual Mind Treatment that is the most effective tool we've found to put Law in motion. Treatment is a positive affirming way to approach any issue. We use the basic principle that what we think about and believe in created in our life, so whether we want greater good or just less bad, the principle works the same. It requires that we consciously decide and think about what we want. It requires that we repeatedly affirm that God is the source of our supply, not Costco.

In high school, we all learned that energy can never be destroyed. All substances can be converted, transmuted, and changed in a million ways, but basic energy cannot be destroyed. It is not God's fault that it took until this past century to convert energy and substance into an automobile, airplane, and computer. The ingredients were always there. Holliwell's point is there was never a shortage in supply, only a shortage of ideas on how to make use of that supply.

Whenever we need something in life, an idea is planted first. The greatest inventions of all times began when someone had an idea to turn a piece of mud or metal into a usable form. At the turn of the century, when people became frustrated that horses were a very slow mode of transportation, they creatively used the materials around them to build the horseless carriage, the automobile.

Holliwell's next point is that where there is no demand, there will be no evidence of supply (47). Why? The secret lies in our consciousness. We will be poor as long as we consciously accept life is a struggle, full of hardship and limitation. Worry restricts our creative abilities. Worry drags us deeper into doubt and fear. When we think abundance, we receive more abundantly. It is not our vocation that determines our wealth, it is the demands we make on ourselves to do better in that vocation that determines our wealth. Mind is a powerful magnet that is a strong force of attraction. The strength of our mind magnet can be charged by constructive thoughts or weakened by destructive thoughts. The choice is ours to make. Supply is always there ready to meet demand, while demand is determined by our thinking.

When Costco becomes our God of supply, it means we believe more in what we see than in what we are thinking. Holliwell wrote that when he needed prosperity, he tried to stay in an environment where there was plenty, and today Costco's good for that. Then he tried to stay in an environment of beauty, which today brings to mind a mountain meadow or river trail. And then he tried to stay around people who felt prosperous, which would be the people in our centers. In this way he used his mind as a magnet to draw in prosperity. It is the will of God that we enjoy our good; that in turn promotes happiness and progress. We must expect that good and only good will reach us, then nothing but good can come to us. When we know this is true, the things that don't appear to be good on the surface will be shown later to be good. We must look beyond appearances and trust in the process.

Our material world is a world of effects, and behind the effects is the world of cause. Everything we see and experience is an effect that started from a cause somewhere in us. The universe we live in is one big chain reaction of Cause & Effect. Remembering this can help us stay on the spiritual path. When our experiences result in more frustration, anxiety, and unhappiness, it is time to wake up and see how far we've strayed off the path.

It is a calculation we should make frequently. And in that spirit of conscious awareness, take a few Holliwell's gems to heart from Chapter 3 (43):

» God did not intend that we should be forever satisfied.
» The Law of the Universe is one of perpetual increase, progress, and growth, so when one good is satisfied, another desire for a greater good develops, on into infinity.
» Yes, it's still okay to wish for that Porsche, but the most important thing to do is believe you can have it.
» There is never a shortage of supply, only a shortage in demand. What are we demanding in our life? What ideas are lying at the back of our mind that we haven't acted upon? Where there is no demand, there can be no supply.
» The secret lies in our consciousness. Don't worry or fret; let go of doubt and fear. Let our mind be the magnet that draws our bliss.

And as my favorite spiritual teacher, Yoda, said, "There is no try; do or do not" (*The Empire Strikes Back,* 2004). Jesus taught us to first seek the Kingdom of Heaven. Heaven is our state of mind. When heaven is orderly, disciplined, and constructive, all things are possible. Each of us is a co-creator with God. Joyfully walk forward into the field of unlimited possibilities.

Chapter 2 2

RELATIONSHIP

TO TWELVE - STEP PROGRAMS

Twelve-step recovery programs continue to be a very popular and successful way to address addictive behavior problems. Practitioners may be contacted by someone enrolled in one of many twelve-step programs available in most communities. Typically the person is not requesting the work of a Practitioner or a client session, but instead will ask the Practitioner to be a nonjudgmental listener as they work through one of the steps. Some of the characteristics of addictive behavior include grandiosity, judgmentalism, intolerance, impulsivity, indecisiveness, dishonesty, controlling, or self-centeredness. In order to better understand the process of twelve-step programs *(Alcoholics Anonymous),* a discussion of the steps may be helpful.

SURRENDER STEPS: ACKNOWLEDGE THE PROBLEM

l) Admitting they are powerless over the addiction and their life has become unmanageable. Only a person being healed will be able to say this; a person in denial will not. Admitting they are powerless frees them from self-delusion. It stops the instinctual reaction to control something that was out of control. Insanity would be doing the same thing and expecting the results to be different. This step confronts denial, which often shows up as blaming, despair, or various control issues. A Practitioner may see this step as coming to grips with reality, the situation here and now, the effect.

2) Recognizing that there is a power greater than they are that can restore sanity. This hands the problem over to God. A Practitioner may recognize this as knowing I, an individual, am not the doer.

3) Deciding to turn over willpower and their life to the care of a Higher Power. This requires taking action and letting go of control without knowing the results. It begins a personal relationship with God.

These first three steps get their bloated nothingness out of the way.

ACTION STEPS:

4) Inventorying their life. The list includes liabilities in three areas: resentments, fears, harm done to themselves and others. It confronts their own character defects and fears, showing how they not only create their own pain but perpetuate it. Through this, they can then outline an ideal situation and know it can be created.

5) Admitting the nature of their wrongs to the Higher Power and another human being. This helps overcome rationalization or fooling oneself. It is challenging because it lets someone else see who they are and what they have done. This is a powerful step in taking responsibility for their behavior, forgiving themselves, and accepting forgiveness.

6) Trusting in a Higher Power, allowing a new start in life to begin.

7) Asking the Higher Power to remove any shortcomings. This includes doing an inventory of their liabilities or excesses, asking God to remove the blocks that shut out the light of Spirit. It is an exercise in self-honesty. Anyone studying Science of Mind may find it easy to stay in denial by refusing to look at a condition. Since anyone in addiction despises themselves and feels very disconnected with their feelings, this step helps get reconnected.

8) Inventorying all they have harmed in their life and being willing to make amends. This action step recognizes they are no longer helpless.

9) Making amends whenever possible, except when doing so would injure oneself or others. This sets up the ability to go into recovery. The Practitioner knows that what people think they were in the past can continue to impact the present. Making amends can heal the past and make running away unnecessary. It shows a willingness to heal their attitude and take personal responsibility. Three lists of amends are required: l) people they can make amends to now, 2) people they can make amends to later, and 3) people they will never make amends to. Usually by the time they are halfway through list #2, list #3 doesn't look so impossible.

MAINTENANCE STEPS:

10) Admitting when they are wrong by continuing to take a personal inventory. It becomes a daily habit that helps build a consciousness that supports their good and gets rid of "stinking thinking." It creates a change in behavior in a solution-oriented way.

11) Meditating and praying to improve their contact with the Higher Power, asking for knowledge of Its will and the personal power to carry it out. This has a calming effect and helps decrease the stress level, allowing the person a more objective evaluation of his actions.

12) Practicing principles in all areas of their life. They are now powerful enough to begin helping others.

These steps are not in conflict with Science of Mind. Treatment and applying Science of Mind principles are not an easier, softer way. Spiritual awakening and overcoming an addiction are both processes. In both cases, there is no magic fix. Treatment and twelve-steps begin with addressing cause. Like any fix, they start at the beginning.

Chapter 23

THOUGHTS ON MIRACLES

Most people think of miracles as events where it appears the laws of the Universe have been circumvented, and something impossible or something that appears supernatural happens. In the Bible, the miracle of the loaves and fishes, feeding the multitudes, and healing the blind were all miracles. For many people, when something that looks like a miracle occurs, it's as if they had no part in it, that God or Infinite Intelligence just took the bull by the horns and forced a change.

We know that is not the case. We know the Universe rearranges itself around our state of consciousness—our consciousness as an individual, a member of a family, our community, our country, and the world. The state of consciousness in the world is very clear from this perspective, which is why metaphysical teachings are so valuable today.

If you have ever driven across country and stopped on top of the Continental Divide, you know it is the place that divides the waters of the whole country into what flows east and what flows west. This is very much like our life. We have our own ridgeline that divides our life into two different dimensions, each full of potential: ONE--our conscious life now; TWO—the world of self-creation where dreams/beliefs unfold with perfect precision, the dimension of the miraculous where the Universe rearranges Itself around our states of consciousness. Every moment we choose to remain focused on what is, we consciously enter the realm of the miraculous.

As a young woman, Mary Manin Morrissey was experiencing the failure of both kidneys. The doctors didn't know what else to do but operate and see if they could figure it out. The night before surgery a minister came to her room and asked Mary if she could believe her kidneys could be healed through prayer. No. Could she believe through prayer that all the poison in one kidney could be transferred to the other kidney and at least one kidney could be healed? No. Could she believe that the minister believed it? Yes. In the morning when the doctors opened her up, they found one pink healthy kidney and the other totally and completely failed. Whereas Mary couldn't believe in it herself, she could accept that someone else believed it (Morrissey 28).

Our thoughts and beliefs flow down the mountain gaining momentum, snowballing, expanding, reaching the critical threshold of manifestation, and it becomes our own personal reality. Form follows thought. For Mary, cause was a new belief and the effect was a physical healing. The appearance of miracles is all around us. In our Center our Practitioners were catalysts for finding organs for a congregant that needed both a kidney and liver transplant; the healing of a baby born with neurological defects; the disappearance of a mysterious kidney infection; finding a place to live, the perfect roommate, the perfect job.

Miracles begin with the simple act of making a decision, which creates a new cause and effect sequence. Our thoughts/beliefs are cause, and what occurs in life are the effects. To change the effect, we must clearly put a new cause in motion and then everything shifts. Nothing is set in concrete. Why? Because we are nothing but energy. Every cell is energy in motion, creating new cells every day. This is the Practitioner's pallet, the energy of mind and body. Miracles are based on the clarity of our intent. Different outcomes are the result of one step, one choice, one word, one thought that changes what we call cause. The slightest change or shift literally makes a world of difference as the flow of energy moves cause into the effect. Our thought energy amplifies our intent.

Visualize a big circle on the left—conscious mind and current experience, our expectations, stating what we want, knowing how it would feel with gratitude, acting as if it were so, paying attention. This is focused energy. Now visualize a big circle on the right—subconscious mind—the seat of long-term memory that knows only to do and does not respond to negative words like "don't." It always says yes. Now above it visualize another circle—Universal Mind—all the accumulated knowledge of every experience in the Universe, which can create beyond our wildest expectations.

It is very important to recognize what we are telling ourselves. A few years ago, I worked with a woman in deep depression from the heavy load of guilt she was carrying around from something she had done. For months the guilt and shame had been gradually extinguishing the life out of her. When I first met with her, she was so shut down she couldn't even take a deep breath. After a few treatment sessions, her family thought it was a miracle when she was able to laugh and smile when she kept her mind in the present moment.

Recently a man who had lost his wife more than two years ago came to see me. His wife had done everything for him. Without her, he didn't know what to do. He had been in a lot of physical pain for months. He told me he was so frustrated he yelled out to God, "No more pain!" and the pain just got worse. As the Practitioner, I reframed the situation using the three circles. The big circle on the left: conscious mind—what are we telling ourselves? The big circle on the right: subconscious mind that only knows to do. The big circle above these: Universal Mind that always is more creative than our mind. Within two weeks the gentleman's pain was almost gone and he was optimistic that he was going to be just fine.

In his book *Healing Words* Dr. Larry Dossey wrote about the spontaneous remissions of cancer after a fifteen-year study of 3,500 people (242). The key findings included

» All patients experienced cancer while **suffering from an additional severe crisis.**
» **Accepting the responsibility for resolving the other crisis** for themselves preceded the spontaneous regression of cancer.
» Each patient took measures to reconstruct his relationships with others, particularly those relationships that had been strained.
» Each person had a remarkable **absence of anxiety and depression** following his diagnosis. In most of the patients their **religious faith was vital** in countering the emotional reactions.
» All the people **gave themselves totally to the will of God** and seemed to sense a larger plan and fuller meaning of life's events.
» The patients **kept a spiritual point of view** about their experience.
(Emphasis added.)

Recognize that our thoughts and beliefs create a magnetic attraction that draws to us like-results in our experience. Use the vegetable garden example with clients. To grow a healthy garden, it is very important to

» Know what we don't want and don't plant those seeds!
» Select the seeds we do want--create our intention. Without the right seeds, we get potluck.
» Clear the weeds, all negative or limiting beliefs.
» Feel what it would be like to have the best healthy vegetables with affirmative prayer.
» Let go and allow the results to manifest--no peeking!
» Don't pull up the carrots to see how they are growing!

The next question that often comes is something like, "Who am I to have this dream or desire come true?" How do we know if a particular goal is right for us? Mary Manin Morrissey says to test your dream with five essential questions (32-48), and if you say no to any one of them, the dream is nothing but a big "I should," and you won't harness enough energy along the path to bring it into form.

Does this dream enliven me? Does the mere thought of it make me excited? Do I feel passionate about it? Living in limitation gradually squeezes the life out of us.

Does this dream align with my core values? If the dream forces me to compromise my fundamental sense of integrity, the end result will be disappointing. When we choose a dream that is in alignment with our core values, Spirit guides us into even greater experiences.

Do I need help from a higher source to make this dream come true? If we think we can do it alone, then we aren't thinking big enough. Spirit sees possibilities greater than our limited vision. Spirit offers guidance that comes in the form of inspired insight, where, if we listen, we will be led step by step. Our job is not to control every last detail, but to let Spirit move through our lives in a more powerful way. This guidance comes through when we are paying attention to Spirit in the power of silence.

Will this dream require me to grow into more of my true self? If the dream is bigger at the beginning, we will grow into it. Every step requires us to grow and stretch so that when the dream manifests, we have grown into a larger experience of life. Big dreams require us to stay on our growing edge.

Will this dream ultimately bless others? Every good and true dream has a seed within it that blesses and benefits others. We are all connected in the web of life, and what harms one ultimately harms all, just as what is truly good for one is ultimately good for all.

If we can say "YES" to all five of these questions, we have established a dream worth spending part of our precious life building. And to many, the result will look like a miracle.

· →➤➤➤ ·

Chapter 24
THE PRACTITIONER AS A BUSINESS

· ◄◄◄◄~ ·

The Practitioner as a business means keeping records of your time, tracking how your business builds, and documenting information for your income tax filing. It also acts as a reminder of the value of daily spiritual practices.

Practitioners are typically required to maintain a log for periodic review by their minister. As a Licensed Practitioner, the logs record our ongoing dedication to service and personal growth and are reviewed by our minister annually for relicensing.

Use a spreadsheet program on your computer to create all the log sheets you need. This is very helpful at tax time, since you will have documented the number of trips to and from the center when you are in service, which are multiplied by the federal mileage reimbursement rate to determine the cost of transportation. Logging payments received from clients is also helpful at tax time. The records also show continuing education hours, which are reported on the practitioner licensing application.

The three key areas of participation for Licensed Practitioners are being active, loyal, and supporting.

Suggestions for Practitioner Log Sheets

Daily Spiritual Practices:
Time spent daily in meditation, chanting, reading, or listening to introspective music.

Sunday Attendance:
Dates of services attended.

In Service:
A monthly calendar showing time spent in service to the Center as a Licensed Practitioner.

SEVA Service:
A calendar showing other volunteer time spent at the Center.

Books and Tapes:
Titles and authors of books read, tapes or lessons listened to.

Classes and Workshops:
Titles of various classes and workshops attended, the teacher/facilitator, and the number of hours in attendance.

Client Reports:
In preparation for licensing, keep written reports on meetings with clients, recording the effect, cause, and treatment focus.

Practitioner Receipts:
A log of all monetary receipts for client work.

Chapter 25

MEDITATION

AND RELIGIOUS SCIENCE

It is interesting that often we do not feel closest to Spirit at moments of intense activity, but instead we find a connection deep inside when we are quiet. Meditation is a powerful tool for expanding the quiet moments when we connect with the sacred, and sense deep inner peace, the joy of life without effort, and make space for answers to be revealed.

Meditation, like many other spiritual practices throughout the world, has not been a cornerstone of metaphysics. Yet while the practice of meditation may not be detailed in *The Science of Mind,* it is mentioned in the text, along with the power of silence. We can feel the strength of Dr. Holmes's opinion about meditation as a tool when he wrote,

> And so we meditate daily upon the Universe of the All Good, the Infinite Indwelling Spirit, which we call God, the Father, Incarnate in man, trying to sense and to feel this Indwelling Good as the Active Principle of our lives . . . for there is what we seem to be, and what

we really are . . . and as we daily meditate upon this
Indwelling God, we shall acquire a greater mental
equivalent. (306)

By using both meditation and spiritual mind treatment,
Holmes was confident that "the one who wishes scientifically
to work out his problems, must daily take the time to meditate
and mentally treat the condition, no matter what the apparent
contradictions may be. He is working silently in the Law, and
the Law will find an outlet through his faith in It" (57). Silence,
meditation, and treatment are a powerful combination.

We comprehend the Infinite only to the degree that
It expresses itself through us, becoming to us that
which we believe It to be. So we daily practice in our
meditations the realization of Life.

Ernest Holmes
The Science of Mind (358)

How do we know meditation will be powerful for us? We do
not know unless we try. So how do we begin? Although there is
no one right or wrong way to meditate, there are an array of
ideas and processes taught around the world that can be used as
guidelines. What did Holmes advise? He wrote, "It is through the
teachings of the illumined that the Spiritual Universe reveals
Itself, imparting to us what we know about God. What we directly
experience ourselves, and what we believe others have experienced, is all we can know about God" (*Science of Mind* 329).
This is how Holmes learned, by studying the teachings of great
spiritual leaders throughout history, the mystics, the illumined.
He felt the mystics were great revealers of the nature of the

Universe and our relationship to God. We can learn the basics of meditation by studying their knowledge, their wisdom, and methods of connecting with the sacred.

Holmes found it fascinating that light comes with an expansion of consciousness. "The light shines in the darkness and the darkness comprehended it not" (John 1:5). This pathway of light that is created through the expansion of consciousness, whether it is through spiritual mind treatment or meditation, is not something we create; it is something that pre-exists and we tap into it. All the great mystics understood this, and the more frequently we tap into it, the greater clarity we will achieve.

Some of the easier-to-understand teachings about meditation come from Eastern teachers. One such teacher, His Holiness the Dalai Lama, teaches the development of single-pointed concentration in his book *The Universe in a Single Atom* (152), which is very potent when that concentration is upon God. The term is used in a general sense to denote practice of any technique for interiorizing the attention and focusing it on some single aspect. In the specific sense, meditation refers to the end result of successful practice of such techniques: direct experience of God through intuitive perception. It is the seventh step of the eightfold path of Yoga described by Patanjali (46), achieved only after one has attained that fixed concentration within, where there is no more identification with the mind, whereby he is completely undisturbed by sensory impressions from the outer world. In deepest meditation one experiences the eighth step of the Yoga path: communion, oneness with God.

> *Superior intelligence was not given to the human*
> *being merely to be used to eat breakfast, lunch, and*

dinner; marry and beget children. It was given that

man might understand the meaning of life and find

soul freedom.

Paramahansa Yogananda
Journey to Self-Realization 265

In *The Heart of the Buddha* Chogyam Trungpa describes meditating as developing mindfulness, which he feels should not be regarded as a minority-group activity or some specialized, eccentric pursuit. Trungpa said, "It is a worldwide approach that relates to all experience: it is tuning in to life" (Gimian 334). This is emphasized in the philosophy of Thich Nhat Hanh, a Vietnamese Zen Master who currently teaches the Four Foundations of Mindfulness at his Plum Village retreat center in France. Here practitioners develop the art of meditating on the mind to be able to see the interdependence of the subject of knowledge and the object of knowledge. He explains that to calm our thoughts we must practice mindfulness of our feelings and perceptions, to know how to observe and recognize the presence of every feeling and thought arising in us. He feels that to receive the full benefits of meditation, we first must build up our power of concentration through the practice of mindfulness in everyday life. Holmes studied the teachings of Buddha, one of the most well-known teachers of meditation, and wrote about him in his book *The Voice Celestial:*

> *Man cannot change the law, but he can change*
>
> *The sequences. The Noble Eightfold Path*
>
> *Will lead to his emancipation, for*

He who fills the stream of consciousness

With Noble Truths and Love shall cause its depth

Of waters to run clear: he shall be held

From pains of guilt, which dying out will set

Him free to enter in Nirvana. (226)

The Buddha realized the benefit of meditation when he discovered that struggling to find answers did not work. Described by Chogyam Trungpa in *Cutting Through Spiritual Materialism*, "We surrender because we would like to communicate with the world 'as it is.' So the practice of meditation involves letting be, trying to go with the pattern, trying to go with the energy and the speed" (Gimian 26).

In the Siddya Yoga tradition, Swami Muktananda explained that one-pointed concentration is used by all of us at one time or another (*Play of Consciousness* 38), such as when we take a test, cook food, or garden. Using this same ability to concentrate our focus on our love for God is meditation, a mind free from thoughts. Another teacher describes it as expanding the space between our thoughts. Through this process we find the place of supreme peace within.

Holmes found Jesus's description of going into the silence very insightful and wrote, "He (Jesus) told us that in prayer we should enter the closet and close the door (Matthew 6:6). Entering the closet means withdrawing into one's own mind. For it is from one's own mind that the creativeness which one possesses emanates" (*Science of Mind* 431). Through the ages this "closet" has been described at various times as the Secret Place of the Most High, the Tabernacle of the Almighty, the Holy of Holies, the place to *Be Still and Know I Am God*.

The term *meditation*, as used by Catholic mystics, often refers to a form of prayer where one ponders Christ. Authors Nick Bakalar and Richard Balkin explain in *The Wisdom of John Paul II* that although in the Christian tradition there are several definitions of prayer, it is most often described as a talk, a conversation with God. "Conversing with someone, not only do we speak but we also listen. Prayer, therefore, is also listening. It consists of listening to hear the interior voice of grace . . . listening to hear the call. And then you ask me how the Pope prays, I answer you: like every Christian—he speaks and he listens. Sometimes, he prays without words, and then he listens all the more. The most important thing is precisely what he hears" (59).

Although types and styles of meditation vary around the world, any practice of meditation can bring us to that perfect state of awareness over time, where we are just one with everything; we observe without judgment; we sit in smiling repose. Meditation also unleashes in us a tremendous level of peace, love, and compassion. Who wouldn't want more of this in their life! Although meditation seems simple, it can be very challenging at the same time, because we grow as our ability to meditate grows.

What tends to come to the forefront of our thoughts when we begin meditating is what is described as "the basic neurosis of mind," which is the relationship between ourselves and our world. As we meditate we begin to understand our thought pattern as well. We can see thoughts as just that . . . thoughts. If we judge our thoughts obsessively, whether condemning or praising, we actually feed and encourage them.

Chogyam Trungpa describes this process in *The Myth of Freedom*. "A person always finds when he begins to practice meditation that all sorts of problems are brought out. Any hidden aspects of your personality are brought out into the open, for the simple reason that for the first time, you are allowing yourself to see your state of mind as it is. For the first time you are not evaluating your thoughts" (Gimian 217).

> *The teaching of the mystics has been that there*
> *should be conscious courting of the Divine Presence.*
> *There should be a conscious receptivity to It, but*
> *a balanced one.*
>
> Ernest Holmes
Science of Mind (329)

Dealing with these thoughts is all part of the process of achieving inner peace. Ram Dass feels it is important to have some understanding what the game of life is about to want to meditate. This popular American meditation teacher explains the challenge in his book *Grist for the Mill*.

> So we have a little bit of wisdom, and then we try to concentrate. But every time we try to concentrate, all of our other desires, all of our other connections and clingings to the world keep pulling on us all the time. So we have to clean up our game a little bit; that is purification, and then our meditation becomes a little deeper. As our meditation gets deeper we are quieter, and we are able to see more of the universe so that wisdom gets deeper and we understand more. The deeper wisdom makes it easier to let go of some of the attachments, which makes it easier to increase right livelihood. All three things keep interweaving with one another; they are a beautiful balancing act. (78)

Some people experience the fear of emptiness or nothingness as the mind releases thoughts and there is a moment when we are not relating to someone or something (Dass, *Grist* 94). Though the fear is not real, that sense of floating without a personal identity causes us to hold back. As the practice continues, we begin to trust the process and ourselves even more.

Many people try meditation to relieve pain, anxiety, tension or sadness. Yet what often comes to mind in the early stages of meditation is the recognition of how protective we are of certain people, places, or things, or the particular way we experience life. Every time we recognize another level of attachment in life, we find our growing edge . . . the next area for more inner work. By continuing to pursue spiritual growth, there will be some point where we suddenly find the hardest work has been left behind. At this point, our lessons are easier and our joy more profound.

Practicing meditation daily until it becomes a habit is the key. As Yogananda so wisely taught, "Habits of yielding to passions result in suffering. Habits of yielding to the mechanical routine of worldly life beget monotony, indifference, vexation, worry, fear, disgust, disillusionment. Habits of attending church and sacred lectures produce fitful inspiration and momentary desire for God. But habits of devotional meditation and concentration produce realization" (*Journey* 266). This is the gift of making meditation a daily habit in our lives.

When we recognize that our Spirit is experiencing life through our body for a purpose, we can find out more about our soul's wants, needs, and desires through the practice of meditation. Since Spirit is larger than the confines of our body, it is valuable to get more attuned with it, so that we can see and understand life from a position greater than what we observe by just being a human being. Our subconscious mind experiences unity with all, contains all knowledge, and is the avenue through which we connect with the Divine. We can access this vast library of information and bring it into our conscious mind through meditation, and at the same time increase our ability to let intuitive thought surface more easily and clearly to guide us on a daily basis.

Throughout the ages, the mystics have taught the value of consciously courting the Divine. Holmes taught that illumination comes as we more frequently realize our Unity with the Whole and constantly endeavor to let the Truth operate through us. Since we connect with the Whole at the point of our subconscious, it will be here alone that we will contact It. He cautioned that perceiving the Self is somewhat like entering a dark room on a bright and sunny day. It takes a while for our eyes to adjust. It takes a while for us mentally to adjust to meditation so that we may experience what lies beyond this physical body and our mind (*Science of Mind* 421).

To assist us in the process, it is helpful to use rituals. Not that a ritual represents any religious belief, but rituals are effective ways to help focus our mind on the inner self. Should you feel any resistance to these suggestions, ignore them, but do not let it stop you from doing basic meditation practices. The most important ritual or step in the process is to find a quiet place to sit where we are not distracted or interrupted. It can be as simple as the corner of a bedroom or study, or in walking meditation using a quiet park, back yard or garden. In sitting meditation, the body position should be comfortable to discourage fidgeting or a desire to sleep. Traditionally this is a cross-legged sitting position with hands in the lap, but you can sit comfortably in a chair or against a wall.

The back is held naturally straight without tension, shoulders back. After taking this position several times, our body and mind quickly begin to settle down when we assume "the position" since subconsciously we have accepted this as the beginning of meditation.

Through rituals the mind will soon begin quieting down as we prepare for meditation. This can be triggered by simply meditating in the same place each day, so that as we approach the "place," our mind recognizes it is time to meditate. Having items around us that are symbolic of our Oneness also trigger this calming effect. It can be anything that reminds us of our true nature, such as a candle. Perhaps a rock or shell from a special place, or picture of a loved one or spiritual teacher will help our mind to settle down. Creating the atmosphere for meditation can include wearing the same clothing, blanket or shawl for warmth. Each time we put on that clothing, the mind will begin to quiet down.

The goal of preparing to meditate is to create a mind free of all thought, yet be fully aware. We let go of memories. We stop creating or solving problems, or dreaming about the future. Our goal is a mind which focuses on the present, not the past or the future. Meditation is the process of reaching the recognition of the eternal present moment. The good news: it is a process that improves with practice. In the early stages, it is natural to watch the mind become hyperactive at the same time we wish it would calm down. Or the mind finally quiets down and just then a thought comes rushing in, we follow it, and the quietness is gone. Noises or bodily functions can distract us. Many things can take us away from the silence, so it is important to recognize meditation as a process that improves over time.

Various methods can be used to pursue the silence. One of the most traditional is following the breath, focusing on each in-breath and each out-breath. This one-point focus helps us reach that place called the "witness consciousness," where we are just consciously aware of our body functions. This helps us to be the observer when thoughts arise, but we do not feel a need to cling to them. We just let them go away. Another method to still the mind is the repetition of one or more words or sounds. In yoga this is called a mantra. Repeating the words "I AM" or a phrase like "God Is Love" can still the mind and open the heart. Chanting is even a more powerful way to open the heart and tap into oneness. Chanting with a tape in a "call and response" fashion, can release tension and build our energy level. There are many chanting and meditation tapes and CDs on the market today. Some are more traditional and a very comfortable beginning for those who want to try chanting as a pathway to deep meditation. The chant can be as simple as repetition of the words "Alleluia," "Kyrie," and "Om Namah Shivaya." Sometimes just listening to a Native American pan flute helps me reach that place.

The length of meditation depends on the one meditating. Ideally, begin with five minutes and gradually increase to thirty minutes a day. If we have the opportunity to meditate one hour or more with a group, it can be a life-changing experience, but for a typical daily practice, thirty minutes is very beneficial.

> *We are trying to get peace or happiness from outside,*
> *from money or power. But real peace, tranquility,*
> *should come from within.*
>
> Dalai Lama (44)

Signs of progress in meditation include an increasing sense of peacefulness; a conscious inner experience of calmness that expands into bliss; finding answers to questions through the intuitive state; increasing mental and physical efficiency; the desire to hold on to the peace and joy of the meditative state; expanding unconditional love toward our loved ones; actual contact with God—with that which is beyond all creation.

Holmes cautioned us not to just meditate for meditation's sake, because he felt that a passive meditation will never produce an active demonstration, any more than an artist can paint a picture by sitting down with his paints but never using them. He felt we should read, study, think, and meditate upon statements which calm us, give us poise and confidence, while erasing all thoughts of fear and tension (*Science of Mind* 246). The Dalai Lama cautions, "It is easier to meditate than to actually do something for others. But to merely meditate on compassion is to take the passive option. Our meditation should form the basis for action, for seizing the opportunity to do something. The motivation of the meditator and sense of universal responsibility should be expressed in deeds" (50).

The result of any spiritual practice is that we are called to action. Bless our life and the life of others, our community, and the world by using meditation as a powerful tool for growth and understanding.

Chapter 26

ERNEST HOLMES

ON PRACTITIONERS

The Ethics of Our Profession

(Stenographic report of lecture on Friday, May 5, 1933)

Whether or not a great many of us ever expect to be professional practitioners is entirely outside of the question. We should all practice, either for ourselves or for someone else. Many will become professional practitioners and will be successful or not according to their own states of consciousness. Here is the only thing in the world that I know of, everything depends upon our state of consciousness.

To begin with, a Practitioner establishes themself in practice not because they work from an institution which has a great background, but because they know how to practice, and practices. There isn't any other way they can ever be permanently or successfully established. If they do this, there is nothing that can keep them from becoming established. It has nothing to do with personality; it is entirely within their own mind and never with anything else. And so if people say to me, "How shall I get established in practice?" I say, "Begin to practice in your own mind and it will not be long before you will have clients." Then they ask, "How are people to know about it?" I do not know how they know about it. How do we know we are alive? There isn't anyone living who can tell us by what power we are able to stand up and speak. Science watches the process of that being and neither science, religion nor philosophy can explain, but has to accept on faith.

Do not feel that you have to know it all. The person who thinks they know it all is a very fortunate individual. If there could be anyone who knew it all, what a terrific position the Universe would be in. It would mean that God would be exhausted or Cosmic Life would die of boredom. There isn't any system of thought or any person who can know it all. Such an attitude stamps a person as being intellectually stupid. The Practitioner, then, isn't one who pretends to know it all. There isn't anyone who thinks that all they have to do is wave their wand. That is not the approach we make to this thing. In fact, that is the attitude that makes this movement queer in the eyes of intelligent people, and we wish to avoid it for the sake of the movement and the good it will do.

The thing we believe in is the most intensely intelligent of any philosophy the world has ever conceived because it is the effect of getting together all the best the world has ever known. The Practitioner is one who is trying in their own mind to see that we are living in a spiritual Universe, disregarding the material evidence which contradicts that assumption; that the spiritual Universe is in harmony; that it is a Unity and is perfect. We know that it does not seem to be so. We know that wherever we look this thought is contradicted by appearance, and we know that appearance and reality are, or may be, entirely different things. Consequently, the Practitioner has a principle to demonstrate and that principle is the harmony of the Universe, the unity of all good, the presence and susceptibility of a dynamic power and consciousness and creativeness which we call the Spirit, ever available and ever present. The Practitioner is one who, in the midst of confusion is trying to sense peace and must begin to treat themself for this condition, as we have discussed over and over again.

As a person who understands these things begins to treat mentally and to know that they are able to help people and that such will be drawn to them, they will find that people begin to come to them for help. That is the way they demonstrate a practice. Therefore, they prove for themself that which they will be able to prove for the other person.

There are certain things that we should know about practice. A mental practitioner of any kind should never put their hands on the client. They can be arrested and sent to jail for doing so. They should never prescribe so much as a certain brand of cold cream. Even casual recommendations that we might make to each other outside of practice, we could be arrested for if we were to say the same thing in the profession. The medical profession is very powerful, very critical, and very jealous of its position and it is well in this case that it should be so, for we do not know anything about prescribing remedies. We are not to lay our hands on our clients or to prescribe any kind of medicine. We are to keep our work in its own field, for that is where it belongs and we should never be disturbed by any other field of action. We should never feel disturbed if the client should go to a physician because it will not in any way interfere with our work. Our work is entirely in the field of mind and we must keep it there. Practice, as we understand it, is a combination of straight mental science and a spiritual atmosphere, and both are necessary. A Practitioner knows exactly what they are doing and why they do it from the standpoint of mental science. They bring as much of the spiritual atmosphere to bear on this understanding as they can conceive.

A Practitioner never talks about their clients. If there is any reason for them to take up the discussion of a client from the standpoint of diagnosis, they do it professionally. Never talk about clients to other clients—that is a very great breach of professional conduct; it is not a good thing to do. Such a Practitioner is not likely to be successful. No one knows whom a Practitioner is treating or why. There are certain ethics about this work which we must be very careful to observe. There is no one who gets closer to people than a Practitioner. Clients tell the innermost secrets of their lives, and it is not only very unethical but also very wrong for a Practitioner to run about and destroy or profane this sacred confidence that has been given them.

A Practitioner is not a pious, narrow-minded person, spiritually and intellectually puffed up. A person who has had the greatest experience in life, theoretically, should be the best Practitioner. A Practitioner is one who, when people come to them, views them neither as saints nor sinners, but just as people. Whatever their reaction to life may be, whatever their habits of living, the Practitioner does not separate them. They view them only as people and cases, but have no opinion about the cases whatever. If they have, the thing they are going to do is subject to that opinion. Why? Because the thing they do takes place in thought, and if they have a pre-conceived thought or opinion about the client, the efficacy of their treatment will be limited to that opinion. Consequently, the Practitioner views people not as good or bad, but just as people, and the condition as a case, which has to be met. There is no class of people who should be so tolerant and broad-minded and understanding of human reactions. Hence, the Practitioner should not discuss with other people the confidences of their clients—it is a dishonest, unholy thing to do. This confidence is a sacred thing and should never go further than the ears of the Practitioner to whom it should not be considered as anything but the evidence of a certain action and reaction.

A Practitioner must never take a personal responsibility for their client. This is a very subtle thing because in order to do our best work, we have to be sympathetic and kindly disposed and yet at the same time we must be very careful not to mentally enter into the state of consciousness, which gives rise to this condition.

There is another very subtle thing about this practice, which is this: If a person goes into it just with the idea of making money, they are not likely to receive it, but if they practice rightly they will get money. In other words, the Practitioner's whole attention is to be centered on the concept of their client or the condition as being in an eternal state in Spirit and manifest in Mind, if they are going to get results. Where our consciousness is centered, our thought and emotions are centered. Our conviction is the affirmative state of our thought. I have noticed in this field above any other (because this field deals entirely with consciousness), that once we have reduced it to a state of thought, then what is going to happen depends on the state of thought. And if a Practitioner's whole reaction is "It is a pretty good thing for me to help this person because of who they are," they had better not try to treat that person. One cannot buy and sell this thing, and one who has the belief that they can is not going to get anywhere by having that state of mind. If a Practitioner, when they come to practice, takes a case for nothing, they must give it just as much time, attention, and thought as if they were being well paid.

There are very few walks in life where a person can become such an unconscious liar as they can in this field. Most of our friends will say, "Now you can treat me." They don't know or care whether or not we are doing it, and we find that within a week we might have fifty people half-believing they are being treated. We would find ourselves swamped. The very first thing we should say to a friend who approaches us and asks for treatment is, "Are you serious? Do you believe in this thing? Do you understand it? Do you accept it? What is your reaction to it?" Explain to people when they do not understand by saying, "Do you wish me to treat you? Do you realize it will take from fifteen minutes to one hour of my time daily?" It is only fair to people that they should understand this; otherwise the Practitioner will make so many loose promises among their friends, that they will become an unconscious liar. It is very likely that unless friends understand, they will think the Practitioner just bunches everyone together and says a good word for them. The Practitioner may even find themselves doing this. Practice is not well-wishing or wishing people well; that is one of the motives back of it, but we have discovered that practice has a definite technique. I wish everyone who studies this thought would realize that unless there were a definite technique, it would not be a science. There are certain laws just as real in the mental and spiritual realm, with which we deal, as there are in any other field of action, and we have to deal with them very definitely in the way they work.

The Practitioner should be very specific. Be very frank, open, and honest with anyone who comes to you, and make them be very honest with you, because people do have a superstitious reaction and think that a Practitioner just says "God bless all of them." Therefore, a Practitioner, of all people, has to be perfectly straightforward, very honest. They should deal with a case not as a personality gone wrong or exceedingly right, but just as a case undergoing an experience, which is the result of the client personally reacting in a certain way to life. The work is impersonal, and the Practitioner can say to their client things that otherwise must seem critical. Be very candid without being critical, and you must be that.

Very few people understand what this practice is; most of the people teaching metaphysics do not understand it. No one's understanding is very great, and many people have hardly any understanding because to most people philosophy is what someone else has taught; religion is what someone else has felt. Too often our religions are our intellectual reactions to other people's concepts rather than our own reactions to an immediate awareness. Therefore, it seems to me that a sincere Practitioner must make up their mind that they are going to spend a great deal of time with themselves, and if they haven't come to the place in their evolution that they can do that, I do not see how they are going to be a good Practitioner, because the work is entirely within oneself.

A Practitioner must be willing, if necessary, to sit up all night with themself, talking to themself. One is not a good Practitioner unless they are willing to do this. Practice is a sacred thing; reaching the most sacred interior of people's consciousness. Never violate these trusts and remain honest and faithful to a client and oneself. We must be very sure in this practice that our motive is absolutely honest and absolutely right. Practitioners are not well paid for their work, they do not make as much money as they could make by the same amount of work in most any other field. They have to concentrate more than people in most any other profession. Like a physician, they are always on call, and unless one is willing to meet these phases of the case, do not go into the field of practice. Fortunately, this field of mental practice is fool-proof—only those people stay in practice who get results, and only those people get results who practice correctly.

We are all in different places in evolution. One man isn't much farther along than another, but one man goes this way while another man goes that way. Let us not let our reaction to this thing be that way. Let us not think there is any person, place, position, influence in life or any opportunism in this work. If our reaction to it in the slightest degree is from the standpoint of opportunism, let us be very honest with ourselves—we don't get anywhere when we do it that way.

Practice is not trying to live another person's life. That is a responsibility we cannot take. Here is what happens: we enter into the state of consciousness, which is theirs and not ours, and that is where we stop. We enter into the reaction, the morbidity, the unhappiness, the fear, and the doubt. But that, in itself, would not be so bad if we did not at the same time enter into the belief that we are responsible for their existence. From the highest and the most sincere motive comes that belief, but that can never be. Therefore, the honest-minded Practitioner must be careful not to get caught in this very subtle trap—the belief that we have to be personally responsible for people. We cannot work right for any person unless we can impersonalize the situation. If we find that we cannot, let us try to work for that person. The moment the Practitioner tries to work that way, they enter into the condition they seek to relieve.

Then there is another reaction, which also comes from the highest motive. It is a hang-over from the old theology that we suffer for righteousness' sake. Someday we will stop doing that—I don't know when. Nothing will have happened except that we will stop suffering and gradually learn that lesson as we see that every person, in the long run, will reach best motive, that it is not our duty to do everything that everyone wants us to do. It is not our duty any more than it is our duty to go out in the street and lie down and let people scrape their feet on us. Right here we should differentiate between a true and false humility.

If this thing cannot be a thing of spontaneity and joy, it isn't worthwhile. That leads us to human elements. Do not be afraid to be spontaneous; virtue is always unconscious; it is always spontaneous. If we can first come to sense that the human and the Divine are the same thing, that the mind we use in our human reasoning is merely as much of that Mind which we call "Divine" as we are able to use, we shall find that this practice of the spiritual life is the most normal, natural and spontaneous thing. And we will find this, that a lot of people who have never heard of metaphysics are much better metaphysicians than we are; and we will also realize that everywhere we look we are going to learn something.

Don't try to make converts. Don't try to drag all your friends in and make them believe. We need to have the convictions that what we believe is so; we do not need to transmit that conviction to any living soul.

If a multitude of men walk down the street and see a granite shaft withstanding the gale, they know it is solid, and if they see a straw blowing in the wind, they know it is just a straw. People are intelligent. In the long run we make an impress on life, which is the exact correspondent of what we actually are.

First, last, and all the time, our whole process is demonstration and that demonstration begins right here. It is the demonstrating of a greater peace in our own life, a greater joy in our own consciousness, a greater spontaneity in our whole expression and a fuller, happier, more successful, and more vital life. People will see things; outside of that we have no mission to convert. Ours is a mission of entering more completely into life for the joy of living. We want that and we shall be a group of people who talk less and do more. Let us practice our belief in our own interior until people see in our daily living the outward result of our inner belief and conviction.

Reprinted by permission of
United Church of Religious Science, 1995.

Chapter 27

WHAT I LEARNED ABOUT ERNEST HOLMES

There is no doubt in my mind that Ernest Holmes was a spiritual leader extraordinaire. Raised in New England in the late 1800s, Holmes did not finish high school, yet he had a tremendous enthusiasm for knowledge and truth and thus was an avid reader of books. Over time he was able to piece together the profound knowledge of many of the world's greatest spiritual leaders and thinkers throughout history. He drew from that knowledge a practical application of Law that works to enhance one's connection with Universal Mind and create positive changes and physical healings in daily life.

Like many spiritual leaders, he found joy, financial and personal satisfaction in his work. Holmes loved being a Practitioner and lecturer. He was a unique spiritual leader and teacher, developing classes, writing texts, and giving Sunday lectures to thousands. Many who followed and learned from him wanted more. In this case his followers wanted him to ordain ministers and establish churches, grow the philosophy and lead a growing organization. His greatest concern was that the teachers and churches would uphold the truths and teachings as he discovered them.

The challenge for any spiritual leader is to maintain clarity while helping those who learn and teach the philosophy to become proficient experts. Any teaching that can improve life as much as Religious Science deserves to be available to all of humanity and brought to the attention of the world. This requires many teachers who use a variety of teaching methods, so the leader will find the greatest growth and strength in the organization by focusing on how to help the individual teachers succeed, focus on the results not just the method.

Holmes gave a twenty-five-word definition of Religious Science: **Religious Science is the correlation of laws of science, opinions of philosophy, and revelations of religion applied to human needs and the aspirations of man** (Vahle 7). He expected his practitioners and ministers to do daily treatment and depend on God first. In healing others he felt the most important thing is to see the Divinity in everyone. He was proud to say we are a teaching order and a healing order, not a preaching order. One of his messages to Practitioners was to do daily treatment knowing every doorway of opportunity is open to us. Every talent and ability we possess is gladly recognized, welcomed, used, and properly compensated for, and therefore we should always have a joyous expectancy of success.

Chapter 28

CELLS AND SUBCONSCIOUS MIND

At an Asilomar conference a few years ago, Dr. Bruce H. Lipton, a cellular research biologist, spoke on the wisdom of our cells. He explained that millions of years ago single-celled organisms started forming colonies, working together, adapting, and changing to survive. Cells formed structured environments to subdivide the workload and cell differentiation increased efficiency and the ability to survive. Our bodies are individual communities of about fifty trillion cells, and each cell has its own life and function, yet each cell interacts with others in a sense of "community." Since health is harmony in the community and disease is disharmony in the community, our health is based on the cooperation of our cells.

In Biology 101, we learned that each cell is a living entity with its own life and function, yet each cell has within it the knowledge to do every function. This is the basis for stem cell research. In the sixties, Dr. Lipton was doing research on cloned stem cells under the guidance of Dr. Irv Konigsberg, who created the first stem cell cultures. When he put genetically identical myoblasts in culture dishes with conditions that supported muscle growth, the cells would become muscles. If he changed the environment, the myoblasts would respond and in one environment they would become bone cells and in another, fat cells. His experiments clearly revealed that the fate of cells was more or less controlled by the environment, completely opposite of the model the medical field had been following for a hundred years that said our cells were controlled by our genes and DNA.

The medical model called *Newtonian physics* is the belief that the body is a machine composed of chemicals controlled by genes and DNA. With this understanding, a doctor looks at the body as a machine and makes adjustments to return it to health. Not only does Newtonian physics see the body as a machine, but the universe as a machine. Scientists felt if they could understand the nature of matter, they could understand nature itself and then control and dominate nature. We are seeing the impacts of that today.

In 1953, Dr. Watson and Dr. Crick studied proteins, which are strings of amino acids, and found they had a backbone, which they called DNA. The strands of DNA contained sequences of genes, which are the blueprints for over 100,000 different kinds of proteins. Proteins are the building blocks that make up a human body. They are shape shifters that respond to electromagnetic charges that generate movement. If you want to know how proteins create life, Dr. Lipton has diagrams and photos in his book, *The Biology of Belief*. It is fascinating.

With the assumption that the body was a machine, scientists felt if all genes could be identified, then perhaps solutions could be found to every medical problem. Scientists estimated the human body would have more than 100,000 genes, because it had already been determined that there were more than 100,000 different proteins in our bodies. In what was called the *Human Genome Project,* scientists studied a primitive worm, which had about 24,000 genes. Next they studied a fruit fly, and it had about 18,000 genes. Then in 2001, they found the human body had about 25,000 genes. This was a shock because the low number of genes could not account for the complexity of a human body. If DNA was the blueprint, but didn't control the cells that have over 100,000 different proteins, where is the brain in a cell that accounts for the complexity of being human?

This next field in biology is called epigenetics, which means "control above genetics," and it is fairly new. So far epigenetics has revealed that the brain of the cell is its skin, the membrane, the interface between the interior of the cell and the world it lives in. At any one time the surface of a cell has over 100,000 different switches—proteins, which respond to a massive variety of environmental signals. The sheer volume is hard to grasp. These protein switches control the functions of our body and our lives.

This is a powerful discovery that is not yet fully accepted by the medical profession. Cells in our body adjust to the environment? How does this work? Dr. Lipton explained in his book that there are receptor proteins in the cell membrane that monitor what's going on outside the cell. When they receive a signal, other proteins go to work to give an appropriate response (53). Now this happens in hundreds of cycles per second. The cells in our body respond to the environment based on the information received by the receptors in our cell membranes.

Our cells are preprogrammed by genes and DNA, but what else sends information to our cells? Our energy level, the food we eat, our thoughts, our habits, and how we are feeling about our decisions and the actions we take, all make up the cell's environment. This is the reason we are all so different. The protein receptors are picking up thousands of bits of information from our mind, just like having a computer keyboard on the surface of our cells. In metaphysics, we look at the primary source of environmental information, our mind, our beliefs, and our decisions.

Dr. Lipton realized that tens of thousands of cells die every day and new cells take their place, yet we still keep living and growing. This realization made him rethink his position as an agnostic and he became a believer in Spirit, in God. It was a spiritual awakening when he realized that the survival of the body is not that important, because our true essence comes from our individual energy in the field of the invisible.

My understanding of how the mind works has also been greatly expanded by the newest guru in the field, Cesar Milan, the Dog Whisperer. I practically inhaled Cesar's book on dog training, *Cesar's Way*, when I bought it. It should not have surprised me when he wrote, "This truly universal, interspecies language is called *energy*" (61). Energy! This is the one thing humans and dogs have in common. Dogs have tremendous sense of smell, but their best trait is their sense of energy. Dogs can sense our energy instantly. Cesar says energy is the language of emotion and dogs can sense even the most subtle changes in the energy and emotions of the people around them (66). Our energy doesn't lie. We can scream at our dog to stay off the sofa until our face turns blue, but if we aren't projecting the energy of a leader, the dog knows the real bottom line. And when we yell, dogs perceive loud talk by humans as an excited, emotional state, which in the dog world is a sign of instability.

In one of his television shows, Cesar met with a couple that were having problems with a rescued dog that was afraid of his own shadow. When they took him for walks, he would tremble all over and walk with his tail between his legs, and bolt for home whenever he got the chance. Cesar showed the owners what he calls "the walk" with the proper position of the leash and how the dog owner can use the power of thought, feelings, and imagination to transform himself into the calm assertive pack leader. He asked the woman what character she could identify with as calm and assertive. She said Cleopatra. When she walked their dog with the energy of Cleopatra, the dog's response changed dramatically. As Cesar shared, once the dog realized he was walking with a queen, he instantly became more relaxed and less fearful. Cesar's mantra is exercise, discipline, and affection. We can give our cells a tremendous gift by doing this for ourselves!

We are actively involved in physically shaping the world that we experience. Energy work and the power of the mind have been known for centuries. In the late 1800s this new way of thinking became very popular thanks to people like Ralph Waldo Emerson, Phineas Quimby, Emma Curtis Hopkins, Mary Baker Eddy, and others, and eventually became known as New Thought. These teachers were the predecessors of Charles and Myrtle Fillmore who began Unity and Ernest Holmes who began Religious Science. Holmes's textbook, *The Science of Mind,* is the core curriculum for four years of study at the Centers for Spiritual Living. We know that our mind is the creative factor in us and its power is limitless. To learn how to think is to learn how to live, for our thoughts go into a medium that is infinite in its ability.

The vast majority of subconscious programming is acquired through our life experiences. Subconscious mind is strictly a stimulus-response device. When an environmental signal is perceived, the subconscious mind engages. Neuroscientists have said that 95 percent or more of our behavior is under the control of the subconscious mind. How can we change the tapes in subconscious mind? One way is to rerecord the program. In *The Science of Mind* we teach the value of becoming more self-conscious and mindful in everything we think and do. According to Dr. Lipton, just thinking positive thoughts doesn't do much (97). Positive thoughts that have a profound effect on our lives are ones that are in harmony with subconscious programming. Negative thoughts have an equally powerful effect on areas where we are negatively programmed. This is why a Practitioner asks questions that help identify what positive and life affirming words could be used to change the programming in subconscious mind. Since our minds are the primary source of environmental information for our cells, let's make ours the happiest, joyous, most loving minds in the world.

· ⇒⟫⟫⟩ ·

Chapter 29

OTHER SPIRITUAL TRADITIONS

· ⟨⟨⟨⟨← ·

A wide variety of spiritual practices and traditions are found in the world today. When looked at closely, many are based on core beliefs similar to Religious Science, but over time new interpretations and traditions have been added so that they often look dramatically different on the outside.

This section presents an overview of the major religions so that the Practitioner will have a basic idea of the various definitions of God that might be influencing the effect in the client's life.

Roman Catholicism

The Articles of Faith for Roman Catholics are found in The Apostles' Creed and the Nicene Creed.

The Apostles' Creed

I believe in God the Father Almighty, Maker of heaven and earth, and in Jesus Christ, His only Son, our Lord, Who was conceived by the Holy Ghost, born of The Virgin Mary, suffered under Pontius Pilate, was crucified, died and was buried: He descended into hell: the third day He rose again from the dead. He ascended into heaven, and sitteth on the right hand of God the Father Almighty; from thence He shall come to judge the quick and the dead. I believe in the Holy Ghost, the holy Catholic Church: the Communion of saints, the forgiveness of sins; the resurrection of the body, and the life everlasting.

We can see by this creed, God is the creator upon which all existence depends. The Church teaches that love is the highest quality that can be expressed in life and encourages total dedication to increasing the good in all areas of life. Since God is everywhere, each individual's life should be ruled by his relationship to God. In general, the Christian life is focused on becoming more Christ-like in daily life.

In Catholicism, attaining salvation is increased by individual confessions of sin and wrongdoing in a confessional at the church and doing the penance (typically prayers) as instructed by the priest. Catholic beliefs include what is known as the Four Last Things: Death, Judgment, Hell (purgatory and resurrection of the body) and Heaven. Purgatory is that state where the soul goes at the time of death, when it has sins "on account" that have not been "paid for" through penance. Each person can shorten his time in purgatory by specific prayers and works, called indulgences. When the soul is cleansed, it enters into eternal union with God. It is believed that at the resurrection, the souls of all people will be reunited with their bodies.

The faith of Roman Catholics is faith in the infallibility of God and thus God's Church. In Church doctrine, the mediator between Christ and the individual soul is the Church. The individual has a direct connection with Christ only through prayer. The Church is the law and personal salvation is available only through the Church. St. Augustine clearly explained the strength of this belief when discussing the authority of the Church when he wrote "Rome has spoken. The matter is finished."

In this teaching, scripture is seen as incomplete and requires the interpretation of the Church to get the correct understanding. To be a Roman Catholic means to have a commitment of faith in the reliability of the Catholic Church, which exists as the Body of Christ. The voice of the Church is accepted as the guiding voice of God and all other sources of truth are secondary. The scriptures are interpreted by the Church, and if some experience or thing does not conform to the voice of the Church, it is invalid.

Protestantism

In historical context Protestantism is considered a fairly new religion since it is only about four centuries old. It is one of the three divisions of the Christian doctrine, along with the Roman Catholic and Orthodox Churches. Protestantism is unique in that it has hundreds of separate organizations, which have different beliefs and a wide variety of practices, yet it is based on the belief that God deals directly with each person and salvation is achieved by faith alone. People are at the center of this branch of Christianity and are expected to express religious faith in their daily thoughts and actions. Although the basic beliefs and faith are the same, over time Protestantism has gained an incredible variety of appearances.

Protestant Christianity formed in the fifteenth and sixteenth centuries when some church leaders questioned the authority of the Catholic Church and the government in those countries where the church and government ruled everyday life. Martin Luther

(1483-1546) is most often remembered. Instead of taking the word of the Church, these men created a new order where people were recognized as individuals, acting on their own personal authority, and accepted responsibility for themselves. Protestants turned away from looking only to the Catholic Church for interpretation of the scriptures and began reading the Bible and interpreting it individually. They inferred that they had free will and were free spirits to choose their own idea of religious life. They felt a direct connection to God and no longer were willing to accept the Catholic Church as an intermediary.

As the Protestant movement solidified, scriptures became the infallible ruling document for life and individual spiritual practices—not the Church. Common to all Protestant factions were doctrines, which included belief in the Trinity, mankind as a sinner, the saving work of Christ, and justification of acts by faith. The test of whether one was a Protestant Christian was one's adherence to these doctrines.

As knowledge and reasoning improved over time, conflicts arose between the conclusions reached by the use of reason vs. the doctrines of faith. For example, one such paradox is that some believed it was reasonable that people are natural creatures limited only by ignorance and lack of experience, while the scriptures indicated people were considered sinners. This contributed to a period in the eighteenth century that was dominated by the use of reason in dealing with religious beliefs and was called the period of Rationalism. It was a new way of thinking that allowed biblical stories to be seen as stories and not accurate historical reports. This enabled Protestantism to be expressed and reflected in the day-to-day life of its members.

Today Protestant beliefs range from conservative to liberal (reason over doctrine) or fundamentalism (interpretation of doctrine) and each has implications in the organization of many churches and codes of conduct. At the core lies this basic thought, as related by the first Assembly of the World Council of Churches:

> Christians are called to live responsibly, to live in response to God's act of redemption in Christ, in any society, even within the most unfavourable social structures.

Judaism

Judaism is a religion with a rich history, most often remembered for the acts of God in the exodus of the Jewish people from Egypt. Jews embody the belief of being the chosen people whom God redeemed, and their work is to keep His statutes as written in the Bible. This covenant is believed unbreakable.

The Jewish faith believes salvation is open to all people in any religion if they obey the law of righteousness—righteous conduct in imitating God's ways and being just and merciful. There is much emphasis on individual action. Life is seen as an arena of moral choices and each person can choose good.

The Hebrew Bible was written over a one-thousand-year time frame and was finished about 1000 AD. It is divided into three sections: The Torah (which includes the Five Books of Genesis), The Prophets, and The Writings. The Bible is a record of the Hebrew's understanding of God, His ways in relationship to the world and all people. It was written by many different scholars, yet contains some common assumptions: God's existence and power; the natural world as a manifestation of God's glory; views of God that range from a narrow concept of God as a national deity to a broad universal concept. God is seen as an imposing force demanding absolute obedience and also a loving and compassionate father who has a close relationship with those that honor him. Obedience to the Torah is the main focus of Judaism. The Mishnah is the code of Jewish law and is the second most sacred book.

Judaism believes there is one eternal God who created the universe and remains in control of it. God is omnipotent and all loving. He created humans as free agents with the ability to choose between good and evil. All people are created equal and should base their relationships with others on love, respect, and understanding. The job of every person is to bring the light of divine unity to every act in daily life. Each person has an individual responsibility to society for its well-being; therefore there must be respect for government and its laws. Life is to be lived in piety and reverence before God and other people. The number one rule of conduct is the imitation of God. Communication with God is done through prayer and meditation. Prayers are a regular part of life and are done at specific times during the day and on special occasions.

In Jewish beliefs, suffering is never perceived as wasted. Its meaning or purpose is often believed to be hidden and beyond human understanding. Suffering is not seen as a direct punishment for sins or error, since it could be the result of sins of past generations. No doctrine of heaven or hell is found in Judaism, only the resurrection of the dead at the ultimate end. That is why living a loving and meaningful life each day is so important.

Buddhism

Buddhism is a religion based on insight as a means of conquering fear and elimination of suffering through realizing the true nature of things. It means "the Teachings of the Enlightened One." The practice is based on purification of conduct followed by purification of the mind, which leads to insight and right understanding. It makes it possible to give up grasping, clinging, infatuation, and dependence on things.

Buddhism is generally thought of as following the way of life of The Awakened One, the Buddha Gotama, who lived about eighty years, around 566-486 BC. When the Buddha talked to people, he spoke in parables, similes, and anecdotes so the average person could identify with what he was explaining. When people choose to live on the path, it is believed that they will understand and appreciate the truth through personal experiences and verification of their faith.

The best way to understand the Buddhist doctrine is to practice it. What is known as the Threefold Path includes morality, meditation, and wisdom, all done simultaneously. The Buddha's principle for life is to find the middle way between a life of extreme sensuality and luxury and extreme asceticism. The real Buddhism has no rites and rituals, manuals or books. It is the practice of the body, voice, and mind working together against suffering. Every aspect is designed to bring knowledge.

The Noble Eightfold Path is both mental and physical. It includes right understanding, knowledge of the practices of Buddhism; right aspiration, renunciation, benevolence/kindness; right speech, abstaining from lying, slander, and idle talk; right action, abstaining from taking what is not given; right livelihood, self support; right effort, positive uses of energy and will; right mindfulness, alert and not overcome with things of the world; right concentration, calm, sure, contemplative, and aware.

Zen Buddhism

Zen Buddhism is only one of many forms of Buddhism and is the best known form in the West. It is not a teaching that comes from scriptures. It originated in China with roots in India. Zen was born during a talk by Buddha Shakyamuni when he declared to one of his disciples, "I have the most precious treasure, spiritual and transcendental, which this moment I hand over to you, O venerable Mahakashyapa." At this moment Mahakashyapa became enlightened. He took his new awareness out to the world and created what is known as Zen.

Around 520 AD, a Zen master and Buddhist monk, Bodhidharma, arrived in China from India, seeking refuge. He brought a special message that lit the fire of Zen throughout the country. He described Zen as "a special transmission outside the scriptures. No dependence upon words and letters; direct pointing at the soul of man; seeing into one's nature and the attainment of Buddhahood" (http://www.buddhanet.net/e-learning/history/bodhidharma.htm). Zen monks went from China to Japan in the twelfth century. The word Zen was the Japanese pronunciation of Ch'an, meaning meditation. Here the practice of sitting in meditation became imbedded in Zen culture and practices. The Zen experience, through meditation, was then applied to the arts and lifestyles throughout society; the Zen experience was to live life in a meditative way.

Zen has none of the typical elements associated with religion. It is not a theology, but a religious path. American theologian and philosopher, Alan Watts, explained it this way in his book *The Way of Zen:*

> Zen is a way and a view of life which does not belong to any of the formal categories of modern Western thought. It is not a religion or a philosophy; it is not a psychology nor a type of science. It is an example of what in India and China is known as a "way of liberation," and is similar in this respect to Yoga, Taoism, and Vedanta. A way of liberation can have no positive definition. (234)

Today Zen training has four main areas: Zazen, sitting in meditation; Koans, lessons or problems beyond logic that reduce reliance on form by using contradictions and paradox; Sanzen, private interviews with the master; Work, physical work that keeps one in contact with everyday life.

Taoism

Older than Confucius, the text of Taoism is called the Tao Te Ching and was written by Lao Tzu. He was born in 604 BC and wrote the text during a period of tremendous political and social unrest. Lao Tzu's beliefs were directly opposite to those of Confucius, who dedicated his life to imposing a moral system that would stop or eliminate the atrocities that had been going on for so long in their country. Lao Tzu wrote the doctrine of inaction or "not doing." This principle means that in human relationships, force only defeats itself. Every action produces a reaction and every challenge has a response. As he explained, a bee being crushed will sting.

The Tao Te Ching gives only conclusions and does not lay out steps to be followed. Each individual must take the steps of right action on his own and the way he see it. This encourages an acceptance of universal harmony, accepting the natural cycles of life such as summer and winter, hot and cold, and Yin and Yang (which governs the behavior of all people). Yin is the principle of darkness, cold, and femininity and invites withdrawal, rest and passivity. Yang is the principle of light, heat, and masculinity and invites activity, even aggression.

In the first or second century AD, the Tao was organized by one of its teachers into a religious structure with monasteries, temples, images, liturgies, and rites, many of which persist until today.

Islam

The prophet Mohammed (born about 575 AD) founded this movement in the seventh century in interior Arabia. Islam is an Arabic word meaning acceptance, surrender, submission, or commitment to a divine ruler whom they follow in every aspect of life. Those who practice Islam are called Muslims.

Islam is an inner attitude of recognizing one's obligations to fulfill the purpose of the Creator. Mohammed had visions from an angel and intense experiences of God sometime after his fortieth birthday. The visions showed him that his mission was to bring God's message to the people. He became a preacher, reformer, and prophet in the city of Mecca for about ten years.

Mohammed's revelations and experiences over twenty years were recorded and are the core of the Muslim scripture, the Koran. His teachings focused on one sovereign deity, Allah, who controlled the destiny of all mankind. Allah created the universe, established its order, and held mankind's fate in His hand. Initially Mohammed placed strong emphasis on the terror of judgment that awaited ungrateful people who refused submission to Allah. The Koran includes vivid accounts of the torments of hell.

The Koran shows Mohammed as a prophet whose purpose was to renew and restore spiritual guidance, not to create a new religion. This is reflected in the opening of the Koran, which is a prayer to God for guidance.

Today Muslim theology considers the Koran to be the very word of God and the highest authority in all matters of faith, theology, and law. It contains warnings; it admonishes and instructs. The Koran teaches predestination and free will and at times emphasizes the necessity to choose whether to obey God. The unity of God is the most fundamental of Muslim beliefs. Next is free will, the freedom to choose and accept the consequences—punishment or reward. It is considered a tremendous act of piety to memorize the Koran.

· ⟶⟫⟫⟩ ·

Chapter 30

HOW THE PRACTITIONER

DEALS WITH

DOMESTIC VIOLENCE

· ⟨⟨⟨⟵ ·

Written in collaboration with Rev. Amy Shukat

Abuse can be found at all levels of society among men, women, children of all ages, the elderly, and even with pets. Abuse affects all sexual preferences and orientations. Statistics are available from websites such as Safe Horizon (www.safehorizon.org), the National Council Against Domestic Violence (www.ncadv.org) and The Hotline for reporting domestic violence (www.the hot line.org). Overall statistics show that in nine out of ten cases, the abuser is male and the abused is female (or one playing the female role); however, this issue severely affects both individuals in the relationship. Until recently, domestic violence (DV) was considered a family affair, and friends, relatives, and neighbors, as well as police and other public service agencies were reluctant to get involved. Due to high profile cases like Nicole Simpson and Laci Peterson, not only is public awareness growing, but new laws and procedures regarding DV have gone into effect.

In Section 3 of the book *Child Protection in Families Experiencing Domestic Violence,* there is a lot of information that would

benefit Practitioners in interactions with clients and congrega-
tions. There are many forms of abuse ranging from a subtle word,
look, or gesture, to violent physical acts. An occasional conflict
in which individuals work out their differences is natural and
normal; however, DV is a pattern of thinking and behavior that
keeps repeating itself and increases in intensity and severity as
the relationship continues. Perhaps even more insidious than
physical abuse is emotional abuse that one individual decides to
inflict on another. Physical violence and the threat of violence
are only part of the pattern. Once physical violence is used in a
relationship, the thought of reoccurrence is never far from mind,
and long term can be just as damaging as the violence itself.

There are at least four million incidents of domestic violence
reported each year and 1 to 3 percent of reported cases end in
serious injury or death. In fact, 20 to 50 percent of all women
in this country have been involved in an abusive relationship,
maybe even several, at some time in their lives. The numbers for
men are even less precise as men may feel more ashamed to report
due to society's masculine stereotypes. Regardless, the shame
and guilt involved cause many cases to go unreported. Domestic
abuse does not discriminate. It affects all socioeconomic classes,
religious and cultural backgrounds, men, women, children of all
ages, the elderly, the gay and lesbian community, pets, and the
list goes on.

One of the biggest myths about DV is that it is caused by
anger. DV has nothing to do with anger—it is about intimidation
and control. It is a conscious choice, not a spur-of-the-moment
decision. Individuals may, however, use anger as an excuse to
abuse. Another myth is that a woman (or someone in the passive
role) provokes this kind of treatment. Not so! It doesn't matter

whether the abused is passive or assertive in the moment of conflict; which instance will set abuse in motion is unpredictable. Another long-standing myth is that drugs and alcohol contribute to abuse. Substance use lowers one's inhibitions to act violently and exacerbates the problem, but is not the cause. Many batterers do not drink or take drugs of any kind. Another fallacy is that DV is all about physical violence. As a matter of fact, the more sophisticated batterers have never—or only once or twice—laid a hand on their victim. It is the *threat* of violence that controls and intimidates the other party.

As Practitioners of the Science of Mind, we know that to heal these issues, the Light of Truth must shine. *The Science of Mind* teaches an aspect of principle that includes the Law of Attraction (like attracts like), so there is something operating in consciousness that attracts the two individuals together. This is a mental/spiritual Truth. At the human level, however, certain dynamics are at work. In approximately 50 percent of DV cases, abusive family backgrounds play a part. Generally, if love was not shown in the home, the children of abuse are often unable to express the love they feel for themselves or others in constructive ways. This can result in either a victim or abuser consciousness or combination of the two. Guilt, fear, anger, frustration, isolation, insecurity, and a need to dominate or be dominated are typical learned behavior patterns. These negative patterns form the basis for how the individual processes relationships. Even healthy-minded and strong individuals might find themselves in relationships with abusive partners and over time, begin to suffer symptoms as well. In cases like these, the parties involved may come from different backgrounds and mindsets, but still find themselves in relationship to each other.

Whether or not the abused grew up in a loving, supportive environment or one where abuse was the norm, low self-esteem is often a result of such a childhood. The same is usually the case for the abusers because they, too, feel powerless in their lives. Feeling like a "victim" of circumstances, they look to control and intimidate others to compensate for the past and feel better about themselves. The abuse causes the abused to feel even worse than they did to begin with, so both the abuser and the abused get caught in the cycle.

There are many reasons why women are more susceptible to DV, such as the "Cinderella Syndrome." Fairy tales teach women to believe that a "white knight" or Mr. Right will one day come along and be the answer to their dreams. He'll be handsome, charming, and perhaps even wealthy and woo her beyond her wildest dreams. This description generally fits the profile of a potential abuser. But contrary to popular belief, abusers generally prey on strong, confident, loving women with strong family ties, not women with low self-esteem. The woman's strength and confidence eventually get worn down after being in the relationship awhile.

DV is not a cut-and-dried issue and even professionals disagree. However, we should remember someone chooses to batter so they can control and intimidate another. There can be many reasons why someone chooses to batter. One is seeing his/her partner as a possession, believing women are inferior to men and holding a cavalier attitude toward abuse or, in the extreme, denying anything like abuse has even taken place. Generally, abused women are raised to be nurturers and caretakers and to "stand by their man." Due to cultural and religious beliefs, many still adhere to old-fashioned values about home and family and consider the man as the dominant leader. Many weave their whole existence around husband and children and lack individual creative expression, which strengthens their perceived dependence on their partner. Additional reasons a woman decides to stay include lack of money, fear of losing her children, lack of social acceptance, and the list goes on. But perhaps the number one reason for staying is fear of violent retaliation if she seeks to leave the relationship.

The cycle of violence has three phases: buildup, escalation, and apologies. The buildup can last days, weeks, or even years. It begins with a lot of demands, rules, and unrealistic expectations, withholding personal freedoms and placing pressure on the abused. There are minor battering instances and/or emotional abuse over real or imagined "infractions" of rules and unrealistic expectations. The abused believes she/he can contain the problem by accommodating the abuser's preferences. However, after experiencing the cycle several times, the abused begins to see her/his behavior has nothing to do with whether or not the violence escalates, because the abuser is in control of the cycle.

In the escalation phase, violence escalates until it is out of control. Tension and rage often result in acute battering. At this stage the intensity, destructiveness, and emotional release are quite extreme. The abuser blames the victim for the violence that has occurred, and many times it looks as if the abused has caused the situation, but, in fact, the batterer has initiated the pattern of violence and has chosen to abuse. This pattern of behavior is confusing to authorities and often results in lack of intervention, which perpetuates the cycle. Then as the abused senses the approach of out-of-control violence, depression and anxiety generally increase, and the abused may even trigger the explosion in order to get beyond it, but it usually just advances to the next phase.

The apology phase is known as the "honeymoon" stage. The batterer becomes very apologetic, loving and kind, promises it will never happen again, and begins to give back to the victim what was previously withheld. The batterer is full of excuses and generally blames outside circumstances like job or money and never really takes personal responsibility for his/her actions. The batterer may seem amenable to counseling and begins to seem like the person the battered originally "fell for." At this stage, when outside help is requested, the one battered is least likely to want outside help and may even begin to defend the batterer. The "victim" really wants to believe abuse will never happen again. But statistically, unless treated, the abuse will reoccur. If the cycle of abuse persists long enough, the honeymoon phase disappears and the cycle goes back and forth from buildup to escalation and back again. After ending an abusive relationship, the abused may reflect that warning signs were there early and they either didn't pay attention or thought they were overreacting.

The following are a few early warning signs of a potentially abusive relationship:

1) **Immediate serious involvement.** The abuser wants to move in together shortly after meeting. This occurs because the batterer cannot hold up the wonderful, loving facade too long before his/her abusive pattern emerges. The desire to move the relationship along fast may seem romantic and reasonable, but it is a possible sign of trouble ahead.

2) **Extreme jealousy.** Jealousy is not about love. Love is about giving to one another, not one possessing the other. It may seem kind of cute and innocent when a new lover wants us all to him- /herself, but it is clearly a means of control.

3) **Isolation.** Abusers work to isolate their partner from family and friends, and avoid meeting new people, or even attending social events in the community. Abusers want the partner to be their whole world.

4) **Hypersensitivity.** The abuser frequently overreacts and becomes excessively angry, irritated, or depressed at even everyday things.

The list of symptoms of distress is long, but includes depression, anxiety, nervousness, low self-esteem, recurring physical dis-eases (such as headaches, asthma, insomnia, back pain, pelvic pain), confusion, emotional detachment (numbness), agitation, chronic apprehension, hyper-vigilance, despair, guilt, shame, fear, and anger.

Abuse is a choice. It becomes a habit whereby two people can become "addicted" to a life that reinforces low self-esteem. Although there are no victims, the consciousness of victimization takes place. There is a subconscious mutual agreement between the two people. The Practitioner's job is to know that this pattern of behavior no longer serves either party, and through treatment, a new healthy pattern can be established in consciousness.

If at any time during a client session a Practitioner senses the client is going to reveal abuse that resulted in physical or mental injury, the Practitioner should stop the discussion and let the client know that Practitioners are mandated reporters and required by law to report abuse. If the client proceeds to discuss the abuse, the Practitioner should already know how to proceed after the meeting, whom to call or what forms to complete that meet the local county or state requirements.

If a client has lived in fear for quite a while and has established in consciousness an expectancy of abuse (from all those around, not just his/her abusive partner), it is important the client know he/she is in an environment of non-judgment. The Practitioner's job is not to rescue people, but to give them the space to think, decide, and act for themselves. Creative action begins when the abused has made the decision to move forward in a new way. Ultimately, for healing to occur, clients must take responsibility for their part in the relationship, forgive themselves for allowing the abuse to take place, and forgive the abuser. Along with forgiveness is personal responsibility.

Spiritual mind treatment is the most important aspect to lasting healing. Dr. Holmes recognized that although one treatment may be all that is necessary, often a series of treatments may be needed for complete healing to occur. In the case of DV, treatment for right and perfect action may need to be supplemented with professional help. Therefore, do not minimize the immediate situation, and have the references and materials on hand to assist the client in finding safety, security, and professional counseling or therapy. As a professional Practitioner, our job is to do affirmative prayer treatment for those who ask and to let them know we support any form of healing. Dr. Ernest Holmes wrote that anything that will help overcome suffering must be good, whether it takes the form of a pill or a prayer and in this case a professional therapist.

As Practitioners, we see beyond any relationship dance that involves violence and manipulation, and we separate the actors from the action. We know the Truth for each individual that the path is open for healing to occur.

The dynamics of DV are complicated and can create a potentially life-threatening situation. All change begins with a desire and readiness to change so, ultimately, the ball is in the client's court. It is not the Practitioner's responsibility to make sure the situation changes; it is our job to trust the Law of Perfection working in their lives. Because the client has chosen to meet, the Practitioner begins with the premise that he/she wants to change, yet recognizes that abusers can be quite proficient at denial.

If clients remain in denial throughout the session, recommend they meet with the pastor or a professional skilled to address their issues. The Practitioner is not trained in psychotherapy, but should be fully competent to refer people to the best local therapists or programs in the area. At the same time, know in consciousness that healing and transformation are taking place for all involved. Release clients to their highest good, knowing peace, harmony, and Divine Right Order and Action.

The greatest gift of Science of Mind is not teaching people what to think, but how to think and make decisions for themselves. The first step in breaking the cycle of abuse is when the abused asks for help. Most do not want to leave the relationship—they just want the violence to stop. The Practitioner's mind must be clear and without judgment about the abused or the abuser. A consciousness of unconditional love must be established before healing can occur.

Rev. Amy Shukat is a licensed minister and life coach and lives in New Jersey. She offers workshops on Domestic Violence that include handouts and a workbook. Rev. Amy can be contacted through LinkedIn.

QUESTIONS FOR DISCUSSION

Chapter 1 – Introduction

1. Explain the Science of Mind principle: We believe in God, the Living Spirit Almighty; one, indestructible, absolute, and self-existent Cause. This One manifests Itself in and through all creation but is not absorbed by Its creation.
2. What is Universal Law?
3. What are the differences between a medical doctor and a Practitioner? Do clients deny the benefit of one if they use the other?
4. How would you explain what the mental cause of illness means?
5. What is meant by rediscovering truth?
6. What will life look like when a client rediscovers God?
7. How can we know the difference between ego and intuition/Spirit?

Chapter 2 – The Concept of Spiritual Mind Healing

1. Explain the Science of Mind principle: We believe in the individualization of the Spirit in us and that all people are individualizations of the One Spirit.

2. How do you explain the concept of unity?
3. Explain three ways to describe the five steps in Treatment.
4. Why do we say the Universe is perfect life, full of love and reason?
5. What are the Laws of the Universe?
6. How do you explain time and space?

Chapter 3 – Opening the Heart

1. Explain the Science of Mind principle: We believe in the eternality, the immortality and the continuity of the individual soul, forever expanding.
2. How does a Practitioner identify someone with a closed heart?
3. Describe a thin place experience in your life.

Chapter 4 – The Professional Practitioner

1. Explain the Science of Mind principle: We believe that heaven is within us, and that we experience it to the degree that we become conscious of it.
2. What are the most important qualities of a professional Practitioner?
3. How is the Practitioner a role model?

Chapter 5 – Renewing Our Heart

1. Explain the Science of Mind principle: We believe the ultimate goal of life to be a complete emancipation from all discord of every nature, and that this goal is sure to be attained by all.
2. What does it mean to be born again spiritually?
3. What is really going on when we are too busy to do our spiritual practices?

Chapter 6 – The Relationship of Healing

1. Explain the Science of Mind principle: We believe in the unity of all life, and that the highest God and the innermost God is One God. We believe that God is personal to all who feel this Indwelling Presence.
2. If the issue the client has come to you with is not one you have handled before, how do you help?
3. What are three ways to explain the Law of Cause and Effect?
4. What should the Practitioner do or say when a client
   » wants to focus on the past or other people?
   » wants a guarantee of change and a specific new effect?
   » continues to have scattered thinking?
   » fears change?
   » does not know his purpose in life?
   » is argumentative?
   » has psychoanalyzed the problem to death?
   » is positive he cannot pay for the Practitioner's service?
5. How do you explain faith to people who think they don't have any?
6. How do you reach a conclusion without counseling?
7. When does a Practitioner tell the client how to resolve his problem?

Chapter 7 – Practical Forgiveness

1. Explain the Science of Mind principle: We believe in the direct revelation of Truth through our intuitive and spiritual nature, and that any one may become a revealer of Truth who lives in close contact with the indwelling God.
2. If a client reveals an effect that shows tremendous harm is being done to another person, what is the Practitioner's responsibility?

3. How long does the idea of karma follow a client?

4. Is it ever too late to change cause?

5. If the inner child of the client is the one you are meeting with, how do you reveal the adult?

6. No matter what you say the client replies, "Yeah, but . . ." What do you do?

7. A client wants you to fix her spouse or friend since they are really the one causing the client's problem. What would the treatment be for?

Chapter 8 – Mental Processes in Personal Healing

1. Explain the Science of Mind principle: We believe that the Universal Spirit, which is God, operates through Universal Mind, the Law of God; and that we are surrounded by this Creative Mind which receives the direct impress of our thought and acts upon it.

2. How do you show compassion yet ask or tell the client a truth he may not want to hear?

3. How far can you compromise on allowing distractions during a client meeting?

4. If a client suggests weekly or frequent meetings with you, what is your response?

5. How do you help a client make a decision on a medical condition, for instance, whether or not to have surgery?

6. When is it appropriate to relate a personal story to help the client see or understand what you are saying?

7. What do you tell a client that is frustrated that her aging and ill parent won't let go of life and die?

8. How do you explain the unexpected death of a child?

Chapter 9 – Spiritual Warrior Training

1. Explain the Science of Mind principle: We believe in the healing of the sick through the Power of this Mind.
2. What do you say to a person who is frozen in fear about the future?
3. When clients are stuck in their belief that there will never be world peace, what do you say?
4. Explain to a student why one should not take four classes at a time in order to be enlightened more quickly.

Chapter 10 – Begin with the Present

1. Explain the Science of Mind principle: We believe in the control of conditions through the Power of this Mind.
2. What does it mean that often clients will do to the Practitioner what they are doing to themselves?
3. Why is it important that the Practitioner be grounded when meeting with a client?
4. Explain karma in relationship to cause and effect.
5. Why is it unproductive for both the Practitioner and the client to be dealing with the same problem?

Chapter 11 – Walking the Razor's Edge

1. Explain the Science of Mind principle: We believe in the eternal goodness, the eternal Loving-kindness and the eternal Givingness of Life to All.
2. Why is it important for the client to be fully present in the present moment?
3. If a client is overly focused on the past or the future, what is likely to happen for him/her?
4. Why are Martin Luther King Jr. and Mahatma Gandhi role models for Practitioners?

Chapter 12 – Looking for Cause

1. Explain the Science of Mind principle: We believe in our own soul, our own spirit, and our own destiny; for we understand that the life of all is God.
2. What do you think are the two most prominent causes at work in most people?
3. What could possibly be the cause for bankruptcy, getting fired from a job, arthritis, an auto accident, breaking a leg, experiencing a perfect nurturing and loving relationship, financial success, a promotion at work?
4. What do you do when a client refuses to look at Cause?
5. What happens when a client refuses to acknowledge responsibility for an effect?

Chapter 13 – Creating a Power Treatment

1. Why is it important to include words in a treatment that vibrate feelings and emotions?
2. Is it important to feel the energy of a treatment?
3. Restate step three of a treatment you have written with the Four Ps.
4. Why is treatment not dependent on God?

Chapter 14 – Aligning the Focus

1. What does it mean that the highest place is in realizing there is no one to be healed?
2. What is more effective, verbal or silent treatment?
3. What does it mean when the Practitioner has complete faith?
4. When is a treatment about the condition and when is it about the client?
5. If treatment works independently of the Practitioner, why should we train to be a Practitioner?

Chapter 15 – Living Life Fully

1. How would you explain the Law of Averages to a client?
2. What did Holmes mean when he said that it is not important that we make an impression upon our environment?
3. How do we determine the success of a Practitioner?
4. How are problems the beginning of solutions?

Chapter 16 - Exercises for Clarity

1. How would you explain the benefits of improving intuition to a client?
2. How important is forgiveness in the healing process?
3. How does the pair of opposites impact a discussion with a client?
4. When is giving and receiving the same?

Chapter 17 – Compassion with Action

1. What is compassion?
2. What are the qualities of compassion?
3. When is our presence an act of compassion?
4. You are asked to visit a client in a hospital. What is your intent?

Chapter 18 – Case Studies

1. How can lack of self-love and unworthiness express in the physical body?
2. Why in Case # l did the Practitioner also have a healing?
3. Many clients want prosperity and abundance. How do you describe what those qualities really mean?
4. What is the most important area of growth for someone asking for treatment for a relationship?

Chapter 19 – Life as I Want It

1. How do you explain evolution on the spiritual path to a client who wants something and wants it now?
2. Explain the seed, the soil, and the plant analogy.
3. What does it mean to create a spiritual prototype?
4. Share your thoughts on what would make up your perfect day.

Chapter 20 – Professionalism

1. What is the value of being a Licensed Practitioner?
2. If Science of Mind is open at the top, could we find out we were doing something wrong or in error?
3. How will you know when you are good enough to establish a successful practice as a Practitioner?
4. If a client sees one Practitioner and then goes to another, what does it mean?
5. What if you have your own problems—what should you do?
6. If a client you did Treatment for loses his job or his relationship, what does it mean?
7. Why is it important to do treatment for your center daily?

Chapter 21 – Staying on the Path

1. What are the daily practices that help you stay on the spiritual path?
2. What does it mean to pray ceaselessly?
3. Why is it that we are never satisfied?
4. What does it mean that if we stick to principle, we won't get off track?
5. How do you explain to a client the problems related to worry?

Chapter 22 – Relationship to Twelve-Step Programs

1. What are some characteristics of addictive behavior?
2. Why is acknowledging the problem a surrender step?
3. In Step 4, a twelve-step program asks the person to inventory his/her life. Relate this to the interview process of a Practitioner.
4. Step 10 invites the person to get rid of "stinking thinking." Relate this to the interview process of a Practitioner.

Chapter 23 – Thoughts on Miracles

1. How do we get started on creating a miracle?
2. How can visualization help to create a miracle?
3. Where does personal responsibility apply?
4. How does the analogy of seed, soil, and plant fit?

Chapter 24 – The Practitioner as a Business

1. What are the three key areas of participation for a Licensed Practitioner?

Chapter 25 – Meditation and Religious Science

1. What is the value of silence in the spiritual practices of a Practitioner?
2. What did Holmes mean, that light comes with an expansion of consciousness?
3. How does one know he has had a direct experience of God?
4. Where does mindfulness fit into meditation?

Chapter 26 – Ernest Holmes on Practitioners

1. How does Dr. Holmes recommend we begin a professional practice?
2. What role does *unity* play in the role of a Practitioner?
3. What did Holmes mean that in the field of a Practitioner, one can become unconscious?
4. Why do we not try to make converts to this philosophy?

Chapter 27 – What I Learned about Ernest Holmes

1. What is the biggest challenge for a spiritual leader in this philosophy?
2. How important is it to follow the methods of this training?
3. What did Holmes mean when he said we are a healing order, not a teaching order?

Chapter 28 – Cells and Subconscious Mind

1. Explain why we believe the body is not a machine.
2. How does our attitude and what we believe affect our prayers?
3. How important is it to understand our subconscious mind?
4. How does our conscious mind impact our subconscious mind?

Chapter 29 – Other Spiritual Traditions

1. What are three core beliefs in most spiritual traditions?
2. What does it mean that we honor all spiritual traditions?
3. What is meant that our philosophy is open at the top?

Chapter 30 – How the Practitioner Deals With Domestic Violence

1. At what point in a conversation with a client does the Practitioner let the client know about mandated reporting?
2. What is the most challenging thing to recognize about physical and mental abuse?

3. How do we teach someone who is being abused about the Law of Attraction?
4. When is the *ball* in the *court* of the Practitioner vs. the *court* of the Client to take responsibility for changing the client's situation?
5. When is it time to refer a client who is abused to a skilled professional therapist or social worker?

BIBLIOGRAPHY

Alcoholics Anonymous World Services. *Alcoholics Anonymous,* 4th ed. New York: Alcoholics Anonymous World Services, 2001.

Bailes, Dr. Frederick. *Basic Principles of the Science of Mind: Twelve Lesson Home Study Course.* Camarillo, CA: DeVorss & Co., 1951.

————. *Healing the Incurable.* Marina del Rey, CA: DeVorss Publications, 1986.

————. *Your Mind Can Heal You.* San Diego: The Book Tree, 2007.

Balkin, Richard, and Nick Bakalar. *The Wisdom of John Paul II.* New York: HarperCollins, 1995.

Barker, Raymond Charles. *The Power of Decision.* New York: Dodd, Mead & Co., 1968.

————. *The Science of Successful Living.* Marina del Rey, CA: DeVorss & Co., 1991.

————. *Spiritual Healing for Today.* Marina del Rey, CA: DeVorss & Company, 1988.

————. *Treat Yourself to Life.* Marina del Rey, CA: DeVorss Publications, 1991.

Beckwith, Dr. Michael. *The Life Lift-Off Cards.* Boulder: Sounds True, 2000.

Bible, King James Version.

Bitzer, Robert. *Collected Essays of Robert Bitzer.* Marina del Rey, CA: DeVorss & Co., 1990.

Borg, Marcus J. *The Heart of Christianity.* New York: HarperCollins Publishers, 2003.

—————. *Meeting Jesus Again for the First Time.* New York: HarperCollins Publishers, 1994.

—————. *Reading the Bible Again for the First Time.* New York: HarperCollins Publishers, 2001.

Bragg, H. Lien. Office on Child Abuse and Neglect, Children's Bureau, Caliber Associates. *Child Protection in Families Experiencing Domestic Violence.* Office on Child Abuse and Neglect, 2003.

Bunson, Matthew E. *Wisdom Teachings of the Dalai Lama.* New York: Penguin Group, 1997.

Butterworth, Eric. *The Universe Is Calling.* New York: Harper San Francisco, 1993.

Carlson, Richard, and Benjamin Shield. *Healers on Healing.* New York: Jeremy P. Tarcher, 1989.

Carter, Craig. *How to Use the Power of Mind in Everyday Life.* Los Angeles: Science of Mind Communications, 1976.

—————. *Your Handbook for Healing.* 4th ed. Los Angeles: Science of Mind Communications, 1991.

Cohen, Alan. *Why Your Life Sucks . . . And What You Can Do About It.* New York: Bantam Books, 2002.

Costa, Dr. Tom. *Life! You Wanna Make Something of It?* Santa Monica, CA: Hay House, Inc., 1988.

Covey, Stephen R. *The Seven Habits of Highly Effective People: Powerful Lessons in Personal Change.* New York: Simon & Schuster, 1990.

Dalai Lama. *The Universe in a Single Atom: The Convergence of Science and Spirituality.* New York: The Doubleday Broadway Publishing Group, 2005.

Dossey, Larry. *Healing Words.* New York: HarperSanFrancisco, 1993.

Emerson, Ralph Waldo. *Emerson's Essays.* New York: Harper & Row, 1951.

Finders, Carol Lee. *Enduring Grace.* New York: HarperCollins Publ., 1993.

Fox, Matthew. *Western Spirituality: Historic Roots, Ecumenical Routes.* New York: Bear & Company, 1984.

Gaze, Harry. *Thomas Troward: An Intimate Memoir of the Teacher and the Man.* Marina del Rey, CA: DeVorss & Company, 1992.

Gimian, Carolyn Rose, ed. *The Collected Works of Chogyam Trungpa, Volume Three: Cutting Through Spiritual Materialism; The Myth of Freedom; The Heart of the Buddha.* Boston: Shambhala Publications, Inc., 2003.

Goldsmith, Joel. *The Art of Spiritual Healing.* New York: HarperCollins, 1992.

————. *Practicing the Presence.* New York: HarperCollins, 1991.

Hedva, Beth. *Journey from Betrayal to Trust.* Berkeley, CA: Celestial Arts, 1995.

Herbert, Nick. *Quantum Reality: Beyond the New Physics.* New York: Anchor Books, 1987.

Holliwell, Raymond. *Working with the Law: 11 Truth Principles for Successful Living.* Camarillo, CA: DeVorss & Company, 2004.

Holmes, Ernest. *The Anatomy of Healing Prayer: Holmes Papers, Volume 2.* Compiled by George P. Bendall. Marina del Rey, CA: DeVorss & Company, 1991.

————. *Can We Talk to God?* Deerfield Beach, FL: Health Communications, Inc., 1992.

————. *Effective Prayer.* 7th ed. Compiled by Willis Kinnear. Los Angeles: Science of Mind Publications, 1974.

————. *The Holmes Papers Volume I: The Philosophy of Ernest Holmes, Volume 1.* Compiled by George P. Bendall. Los Angeles: South Bay Church of Religious Science, 1989.

————. *How to Use the Science of Mind.* New York: Dodd, Mead & Company, 1951.

————. *Ideas of Power: Holmes Papers, Volume 3.* Compiled by George P. Bendall. Marina del Rey, CA: DeVorss & Company, 1992.

————. *Lessons in Spiritual Mind Healing.* 1943. Los Angeles: United Church of Religious Science, 7th printing 1971.

————. *Living the Science of Mind.* Marina del Rey, CA: DeVorss Publications, 1984.

————. *Love and Law: The Unpublished Teachings.* Edited by Marilyn Leo. New York: Jeremy P. Tarcher/Putnam, 2001.

————. *Prayer: How to Pray Effectively from the Science of Mind.* New York: Jeremy P. Tarcher/Penguin, 2008.

————. *The Science of Mind.* 50th anniversary ed. New York: G. P. Putman's Sons. 1988.

Holmes, Ernest, and Willis Kinnear. *Practical Application of Science of Mind.* Los Angeles: Science of Mind Publications, 1987.

Hopkins, Emma Curtis. *Scientific Christian Mental Practice.* New York: Cosimo Classics, 2009.

Ingraham, E.V. *Wells of Abundance.* Marina del Rey, CA: DeVorss & Company, 1966.

Jeffery, H. B. *The Principles of Healing.* Ft. Worth, TX: Christ Truth League, 1994.

Kant, Immanuel. *The Critique of Pure Reason.* Trans. by J. M. D. Meiklejohn. Seattle: Pacific Publishing Studio, 2011.

King, Dr. Martin Luther, Jr., "Nonviolence." *Christian Century Journal.* no. 74 (1957) 158-167.

Kubler-Ross, Elisabeth. *On Death and Dying.* New York: Macmillan Publishing Co., 1969

LeMance, Ken. *Professional Malpractice.* http://www.legalmatch.com/law-library/article/professional-malpractice.html

Lipton, Dr. Bruce. *The Biology of Belief.* Carlsbad, CA: Hay House, Inc., 2005.

Milan, Cesar. *Cesar's Way: The Natural, Everyday Guide to Understanding & Correcting Common Dog Problems.* New York: Harmony Books, 2006.

Miller, Ruth. *Unveiling Your Hidden Power.* Beaverton, OR: Wise Woman Press, 2005.

Moore, Thomas. *Care of the Soul.* New York: HarperCollins Pub., 1991.

Morrissey, Mary Manin. *Building Your Field of Dreams.* New York: Bantam Books, 1997.

Muktananda, Swami. *Play of Consciousness: A Spiritual Autobiography.* South Fallsburg, New York: SYDA Foundation, 1994.

O'Neal, David. *Meister Eckhart, From Whom God Hid Nothing: Sermons, Writings, & Sayings.* Boston: New Seeds Books, 1996.

Patanjali. *How to Know God: The Yoga Aphorisms of Patanjali.* Translated by Swami Prabhavananda and Christopher Isherwood. Hollywood: Vendanta Press, 2007.

Peck, M. Scott. *The Different Drum: Community Making and Peace.* 1988. New York: Touchstone, 1998.

Prabhu, R. K. and U. R, Rao, eds. *The Mind of Mahatma Gandhi.* Ahmedabad, India: Navajivan Publishing House. 2010.

Ram Dass and Paul Gorman. *How Can I Help?* New York: Alfred A. Knopf, Inc., 1985.

Ram Dass and Stephen Levine. *Grist for the Mill.* 1976. Berkeley, CA: Celestial Arts, 1987.

Rinpoche, Sogyal. *The Tibetan Book of Living and Dying.* New York: Harper Collins, 1992.

Schmidt, Helmut. "Can an Effect Precede Its Cause?" *Foundations of Physics,* June 1978, 463-480.

Schultz, J. Kennedy. *A Legacy of Truth.* Atlanta: Brob House Books, 1987.

Star Wars, Episode V, The Empire Strikes Back. Lucasfilm Ltd, 2004

TenBrook, Gretchen W. *Broken Bodies, Healing Hearts: Reflections of a Hospital Chaplain.* New York: Haworth Pastoral Press, 2000.

Troward, Thomas. *Bible Mystery and Bible Meaning.* New York: G. P. Putnam's Sons, 1988.

————. *The Creative Process in the Individual.* 1915. Marina del Rey, CA: DeVorss & Co. 1991

————. *The Edinburgh Lectures & Dore Lectures on Mental Practice.* Marina del Rey, CA: DeVorss & Company, 1989.

————. *The Law and The Word.* 1917. New York: Dodd, Mead & Co., 1940;

Vahle, Neal. *Open at the Top: The Life of Ernest Holmes.* Mill Valley, CA: Open View Press, 1993.

Vanzant, Iyanla. *Acts of Faith, Daily Meditations for People of Color.* New York: Fireside, 1993.

Vardey, Lucinda. *Mother Teresa: A Simple Path.* New York: Ballentine Books, 1995.

Washington, James M., ed. *A Testament of Hope: The Essential Writings and Speeches of Martin Luther King, Jr.* New York: Harper San Francisco, 1986.

Waterhouse, Dr. John B. *5 Steps to Freedom: An Introduction to Spiritual Mind Treatment.* Camarillo, CA: DeVorss & Company, 2003.

Watts, Alan. *The Way of Zen.* 1957. New York: Vintage Books, 1985.

Williamson, Marianne. *A Return to Love: Reflections on the Principles of A Course in Miracles.* 1992. New York: HarperCollins, second printing 1996.

Yogananda, Paramahansa. *Journey to Self-Realization.* Los Angeles: Self-Realization Fellowship, 1997.

————. *Where There Is Light: Insight and Inspiration for Meeting Life's Challenges.* Los Angeles: Self-Realization Fellowship, 1988.

Zukav, Gary. *The Seat of the Soul.* New York: Fireside, 1990.

·　→≫≫▶　·

A B O U T   T H E   A U T H O R

·　◀≪≪←　·

Rev. Mary E. Mitchell

Mary Mitchell's destiny was launched with a degree in Forest Industries Management from The Ohio State University followed by a long career in the wood products, pulp and paper, and wood-fired power industries in the Pacific Northwest and Northern California. Her interest in metaphysics was pivotal to her success in industry and the last decade of her career managing a resource conservation district.

Soon after moving to California, Mary found her spiritual home at the Center for Spiritual Living, Redding (previously the Redding Church of Religious Science) where she began classes in the Science of Mind philosophy. This propelled her into deeper study, which was supported by her love of writing. She was licensed as a Religious Science Practitioner in 1993, a Minister in 2003, and was ordained in 2008.

When she retired from the conservation district at the end of May 2012, the next week she was asked to serve as interim co-pastor at the 325-member Center in Redding until a new pastor was hired. She thought that a short stint as co-pastor would be only a small deviation from full retirement. Two years later, what

213

she didn't expect was the impact her lessons on the science of our mind and our relationship with Infinite Intelligence would turn into life-changing experiences for the congregation plus two new books and the third edition of this book.

This edition is a natural follow-up to Mary's previous publications (written under Mary E. Schroeder): *Jump into Life* with James Golden; *The Practitioner Handbook* (first and second editions); and *Engaging Grace: How to Use the Power of Co-Creation in Daily Life.* The new books being launched on www.amazon.com are *32 Easy Lessons in Metaphysics and the Science of Our Mind* and *The History of the Center for Spiritual Living, Redding 1971-2014.* Every day Mary is inspired by the lake, mountains, and wildlife around her home in Cottonwood, California, where she lives with her wonderfully supportive husband, Paul Mitchell, and their persnickety cat, Max.